AF594735

COMPOUND IMPACT

The New Era of Financial Guidance

By

AMY SALO

Ballast Books, LLC
www.ballastbooks.com

ISBN: 978-1-964934-03-7

Printed in the Hong Kong

Published by Ballast Books
www.ballastbooks.com

For more information, bulk orders, appearances, or speaking requests, please email: info@ballastbooks.com

TABLE OF CONTENTS

FOREWORD

by Farshad Asl

Compound Impact acts as both a mirror and a map, offering a comprehensive blueprint filled with real-life wisdom for anyone in financial services—or any entrepreneurial endeavor. Through frank and authentic narration, Amy Salo transitions from an advisor to a trusted mentor and leader, advocating passionately for a career defined by ethical conduct and sincere engagement.

Amy Salo, a good friend, a great leader, and an amazing mentor for many, revolutionizes your perception of what it truly means to be a trusted advisor with incisive clarity and compelling insights. She explores the foundational principles that are pivotal to every advisor's practice: fostering trust and prioritizing the genuine well-being of clients.

In this transformative book, Amy extends beyond conventional strategies to the very heart of our profession. She articulately underscores that while our work may be quantified through numbers and transactions, its true significance is rooted in the human connections we establish and the profound impacts we have on clients' lives.

Amy's steadfast focus on integrity is especially notable as she illustrates how the most effective advisors do more than perform transactions; they cultivate enduring relationships grounded in mutual respect and trust. These connections not only achieve professional objectives but also create extensive networks of personal and professional contacts that endure well beyond ordinary business dealings.

Compound Impact is an indispensable resource for those ready to alter their approach to business and leadership. It promises not just to refine your professional practices but to fundamentally transform how you view and engage in your role within your community and the broader industry.

To all aspiring leaders, advisors, and entrepreneurs: get ready to be challenged, inspired, and transformed. Remember, true leadership is about more than achieving success—it's about making a meaningful difference in the lives of others, and *Compound Impact* will guide you every step of the way.

—**Farshad Asl**, Amazon best-selling author of four books, renowned leadership expert, regional director at Bankers Life, and esteemed speaker

INTRODUCTION

"How do you reconcile who you are as a person with the profession you're in?"

Ouch.

This gut punch of a question came from my Uncle Leo, who knows me about as well as my own parents do. A man who, in his nineties, remains an avid reader and history buff—not to mention my daily online Scrabble partner.

I am not a crooked loan shark, slimy used car salesperson, or ambulance-chasing billboard lawyer. I am a financial advisor.

If you're reading this book, you may be one too—so you know what I'm talking about. The reputation of our industry ranks not much higher than the stereotypes listed above.

Let's face it: Public perception of financial advisors has tanked. Our clients may love us,[1] but the public sure doesn't.

---

[1] The J.D. Power 2024 U.S. Full-Service Investor Satisfaction Study found an eight-point annual increase in self-reported satisfaction among investors working with financial advisors: "Satisfaction Rises among Clients Using Financial Advisors," *The Wealth Advisor*, March 21, 2024, https://www.thewealthadvisor.com/article/satisfaction-rises-among-clients-using-financial-advisors. This supports the findings of a 2021 Consumer Financial Behaviors Study by Herbers & Company that Americans working with a financial advisor were nearly twice as likely to report higher on "predictors" of happiness: gratefulness, intention, impact, & fulfillment: Patrick Donachie, "New Study Finds Clients Using Financial Advisors Are Happier," Wealth Management.com, December 7, 2021, https://www.wealthmanagement.com/industry/new-study-finds-clients-using-financial-advisors-are-happier.

Americans still want financial advice, but they'd rather turn to family and friends—not to mention Google, TikTok, and other digital platforms—than hire a professional. Only 32 percent of Americans seek help from a financial advisor. More than half of Americans turn to family, and 40 percent look for tips on social media, podcasts, or videos.[2]

Some of the loudest voices—whether television financial personalities or social media influencers—have no relevant licenses and no experience creating personalized financial plans for individual clients. They simply rattle off some generic disclaimer, then say whatever they want—no matter how under-researched, unfounded, or sensational.

As a professional who trained hard for your licenses and those letters behind your name, you're right to be alarmed. If these trends continue, fewer Americans will get the help they need to improve their finances, public trust in advisors will continue to degrade, and we will go the way of Blockbuster.

Evolution—or Extinction

Why do Americans regard trained, certified advisors with such suspicion while putting so much faith in social media influencers, television personalities, and under-informed friends, cousins, and in-laws?

Back in 2015, another Harris poll found that 71 percent of Americans find aspects of talking to financial advisors "scary,"

[2] Based on a 2022 online survey conducted by financial advisory fintech Intelliflo and The Harris Poll: Kat Tretina, "You Should Get A Financial Advisor," *Forbes* Advisor, August 17, 2023, https://www.forbes.com/advisor/investing/financial-advisor/you-should-get-a-financial-advisor/.

with nearly half concerned that professional advising "will end up costing me a lot of money."[3]

Since then, the situation has only gotten worse. The American public increasingly associates professional advisors with high fees; aggressive, self-interested product-pushing; complex jargon; and conflicts of interest related to commissions.

To be fair, many industry patterns support this view of advisors as predatory sharks out for our own gain. Too often, firms celebrate product sales while failing to incentivize customized, comprehensive planning focused on maximizing client security and wealth over the long term.

When, as industry leaders, we give awards based on sales numbers, it's no wonder so many advisors take a traditional—that is, *transactional*—approach driven by short-sighted personal gain. In so doing, we fail to establish sincere, foundational trust with clients, engage with their communities, or innovate changes within the field that could deeply benefit our clients.

It also helps explain why we fail to hold on to advisors, with an average four-year retention rate of just 15 percent,[4] not just for individual firms, but for the industry at large. It's no wonder advisors tend to burn out and drop out, considering our culture of sales quotas and fierce competition, not to mention training practices trapped in the 1950s.

---

[3] Conducted by Philadelphia-based financial advising firm, McAdam: "2015 Harris Poll RQ® Summary Report," Skift, February 2015, https://skift.com/wp-content/uploads/2015/02/2015-RQ-Media-Release-Report_020415.pdf.

[4] According to a 2020 LIMRA and Finseca survey: Kathleen Krozel, "A Path To Better Agent Retention," *InsuranceNewsNet* Magazine, June 1, 2022, https://insurancenewsnet.com/innarticle/a-path-to-better-agent-retention.

Shark tanks make for entertaining television, but they won't attract the right people to our field. We need leaders and advisors with a genuine interest in building relationships through meaningful, long-term financial guidance that enriches clients and families in ways that ripple out into our communities.

The result of our inability to evolve is a wholly unimpressive impact in relation to our potential as advisors, as leaders, and as an industry at large.

We can't get where we need to go by hanging out in the dinosaur graveyard. Let's instead begin by meeting the public where they are (and it's not there).

Earning Trust

There are lots of reasons why more Americans don't get the financial care they need. Emerging technology plays a role. So does the common, misguided assumption that people can't afford or benefit from an advisor until they've already accumulated considerable wealth.

But the main problem goes beyond misinformation and lack of public savvy. The problem is a deficit of trust in us. This won't be solved by every member of the public becoming their own advisor. That's about as reasonable as expecting every patient to earn a medical degree to treat their own colds.

Government regulations certainly won't save us. If anything, these efforts further erode public trust in our field, widening the American public's trillion-dollar savings deficit and leaving people vulnerable to the devastating losses resulting from unexpected life events without proper planning.

This has to be solved by a real, genuine transference of trust. As advisors, we do that by truly putting our clients' best interests first—not just *saying* we do.

We do it by listening with the intent to understand, and then developing financial plans best suited to boost our clients' long-term financial health, according to their specific goals and circumstances.

Most importantly, we do it by measuring our success based on the optimal impact we can have on our clients, their families, and our communities. This, in turn, leads to lifelong client relationships and referrals that help our businesses grow.

Recently an advisor called me for guidance. "I need your help," she said. "I have a client in his twenties, earning $80,000 a year. He's been doing his own financial planning, decided it's not working, and wants help. But here's the thing: He insists that he doesn't want to be *sold* anything. What should I say?"

This aversion to "being sold" something makes sense. Considering that many financial advisors still measure their success in terms of product sales, I get it.

Let's look beyond the sales to impact. We've all seen clients take our lead and enrich their lives through properly managed savings and investment plans. We've also seen them ignore our advice, say to purchase disability insurance, only to end up financially ruined by an unexpected, debilitating accident or illness.

We've seen the basic safety and security offered by a solid life insurance payout soften the blow of unbearable loss. And we've seen what happens otherwise—how perfectly avoidable financial hardships can compound tragic loss and devastate families.

We've seen compound interest on a healthy savings habit help people of modest means put their kids through college without student loans.

We know how our work can change lives, as well as the reality that sales are a part of that—as long as we actually align those to *client interests*. Not short-term sales goals for meaningless company awards.

My answer was simple. I said, "Tell him this: 'If you want to do it yourself, I can guide you to some of the better literature and online resources. If you want to work with us, we're going to recommend life and disability insurance. We're going to set up an automated savings strategy for investing your money. We're going to suggest other products, as appropriate, to match your personalized needs—and we are going to sell these things to you.'"

She came back to me and said, "I can't believe it. It went so well. He just said, 'Oh, that makes sense. I guess I do want your help.'"

As leaders, we have to help advisors understand how to honestly, transparently, and logically explain what we do, how we do it, and why—within a business that has not always done things the right way.

In putting clients first, we align products with their goals and help ensure the most powerful outcomes.

Good Outcomes = Good Business

Providing the best possible guidance to those we're meant to serve is not some virtue-signaling, do-gooder impulse.

It's *good business.*

You won't build mutually profitable long-term client relationships with a culture based on short-term sales goals. You also won't retain advisors by depriving them of proper training and support, then pitting them against each other through arbitrary goals and gamified competitive tactics.

Our industry failures lead to costly client attrition and advisor turnover. As we increasingly struggle to attract consumers and recruit talent in the first place, we can no longer afford to maintain the status quo.

To thrive moving forward, advisors need to get more authentic—more *real*—and so do we, as industry leaders. Because if leaders change, advisors will too.

Optimally, our profession would be viewed much more like the medical profession. Having a primary care advisor would be the norm, with the goal of achieving optimal financial health.

To do this, we need professionals who are both others-focused and results-oriented. Advisors and leaders who care about the impact of their work efforts and communicate recommendations in ways that build trust and inspire action. Leaders who understand the gravity of their position and appreciate the ripple effects of their impact—for good or ill—depending on whether or not clients trust our advisors enough to take their advice.

If we meet our consumers, clients, and advisors where they are, and we truly focus on their successes, we will help everyone in a more holistic way, gaining trust and access earlier and optimizing our impact for generations to come.

My Background

After nearly twenty years in the business, I've worn just about every hat in the industry, providing financial guidance to hundreds of clients over these years, and recruiting, training, and mentoring hundreds of advisors. I also advocate this consumer-centric approach to financial guidance through podcasts, industry publications, and both national and international speaking engagements.

Now a managing partner at a prominent New York financial group, I remain dedicated to changing how we do business—both in my own firm and in my role chairing the Finseca Board of Directors Advocacy Committee, as well as its Standards of Conduct Committee.

Our firm, Forest Hills Financial Group, fosters a culture that attracts, nurtures, and retains a diverse group of dedicated advisors, all aimed at ensuring that the next generation prospers more than the last. This approach serves our clients and communities, and also helps our team thrive and grow. With about one hundred career agents and more than 30,000 clients, we boast a wide reach and an advisor retention rate over 50 percent—and we won't stop until we surpass 70 percent. I'm fortunate to work with partners who will never accept the status quo as good enough.

In addition to these industry creds, I was trained in a decidedly unconventional way—at least, compared to most of my colleagues. Before becoming a Certified Financial Planner (CFP), Business Exit Planner (CExP), Chartered Advisor in Philanthropy (CAP), and Retirement Income Certified Professional (RICP), I earned my bachelor's and master's degrees . . . in trombone performance.

When I came to financial advising in my late twenties, I'd worked as a professional trombonist and single mom—a far cry from the finance majors and salespeople our field usually attracts. I had progressed far enough in my career as a trombonist to determine that there were qualities in the very best musicians that I knew I didn't possess. If I was going to make a change, I needed a career with unlimited growth opportunities, the ability to have a real impact, and most importantly one that didn't require me to complete more degrees before I could get started.

At first, it didn't feel like the financial business was built for people like me. I'll never forget one morning when my son, Calvin, was a toddler, and I had to hustle to make it to my 8:30 a.m. training session.

To make it on time, I first drove to drop off my son at daycare as soon as their doors opened, then darted away, with no time to ease my mind or heart by watching his tantrum resolve through the one-way mirrored window. I quickly dropped off my car, hopped a train into the city, then sprinted to my office—only to be locked out of the training session for arriving at 8:35 a.m.

Despite my best efforts and two hours of frantic hustle, I missed my training by five minutes.

"Luckily" (so they presented it to me), I was allowed to skip these regular morning sessions due to "extenuating circumstances."

This made less than no sense. What's the point of holding sessions of in-person training so early in the day with such a rigid late policy? How is *having a kid* an "extenuating circumstance"?

This lack of flexibility was clearly by choice, not by necessity, and it reflected outdated values and unexamined assumptions about who should, and could, work in this field—which clearly did not include single parents. Such inflexibility almost guarantees narrow industry demographics, attracting and supporting only those who already enjoy enough privilege and support to get past the industry gatekeepers and play by arbitrarily strict rules.

Most bewildering of all, it seemed that I was supposed to interpret missing my training as a "win."

Determined not to cheat myself, I looked for whatever resources I could find to be trained—not only to make up for what I'd missed, but also to supplement normal sessions with additional training.

Within a year and half, I began ad-hoc training my colleagues—and set myself on a path to help reimagine, reposition, and revolutionize a new era of financial guidance.

Financial Guidance for a Better Future

Sharks may seem impressive, intimidating, and in charge of their destiny, but they tend to follow the same migratory patterns every year—that is, until they get stuck in a net, run over by a propeller, or eaten by one of their own. While their evolutionary adaptations, rooted millions of years in the past, helped create apex predators, they're certainly not advantageous within non-predatory exchanges.

No naturalist ever marveled over the collaborative dynamics of shark culture. Venture capitalist-types may love the image of "keep closing (and growing your quarterly bottom line) or DIE," but let's agree—it's not exactly a balanced, others-centered way to approach life or work.

If you can't tell by now, this book does not take an advisor-first, client-second "shark" approach to the business. It's also not about taking a stance on any particular investment, insurance, or financial planning strategy.

Instead, it's about building a truly consumer-first philosophy of financial guidance, one driven by how we interact with our clients, advisors, and our profession as a whole. One for students of the business committed to life-long growth and the belief that we can build lasting, fulfilling careers—while building a better future for everyone.

We'll talk about how to center the consumers we reach out to, clients we work with, and advisors we recruit, train, and mentor. How to meet these individuals where they are, and move them toward a more impactful future, with greater success for everyone.

We do that by asking better questions:

> *What is the most our profession can accomplish—for a particular client and in general?*
>
> *Who do we need in the business to accomplish this? How do we need to show up to attract those people, and how do we support and guide them?*
>
> *How can we build trust with the public so we can help them best protect and grow their assets for themselves and future generations?*

We'll review small steps anyone in our business can take right now to start an evolution—or even revolution—that transforms how consumers view, engage with, and benefit from our profession.

We do this by becoming authentically others-focused. That means examining our core drive and earning client trust, engaging with our communities, and innovating industry changes that lead to positive *compound impact*—for everyone involved.

This book is for my Uncle Leo and for anyone else who's fairly sure the financial industry is out to screw them but can't exactly put their finger on how—or what to do about it.

It's for financial advisors trying to figure out why people don't just trust them or take their advice, even though it's obvious their spreadsheets are right. For financial leaders stuck in a vicious loop of *this is how it has always been done*—who can't stop hitting their heads against a brick wall long enough to realize the world has moved on.

Finally, it's for every American who still believes in the American Dream and would be willing to accept our help if we're willing to lead the change.

I agree. We have to change. I hope this book helps move the needle even one percent.

CHAPTER 1

DRIVE *for* ADVISORS

One of the most resonating tips I give new financial advisors originally came from my undergraduate trombone professor.

During my junior year as a trombone performance major at the University of Hartford's Hartt School of Music, I designed and performed a forty-five-minute solo concert. Since the concert was an official measure of my progress, I selected challenging music and worked very hard to prepare. (In those days, with my entire focus on perfecting this craft, "working hard" meant practicing five hours a day, in addition to classes and rehearsals.)

I felt quite proud after this first full-length solo performance. During my next weekly session with my trombone professor, private instructor, and mentor, I eagerly asked, "What did you think?"

"It was okay," came his nonchalant reply. (The man famously didn't mince words.)

Okay??? Obviously this was not the response I wanted. When I swallowed my pride and asked what I could have done better, he said something I'll never forget:

"You need to hang your ears on the end of your bell."

Even to a trombone major, his response didn't make much sense at first—so if you're scratching your head, stay with me. If you held a trombone (the one with that long slide) and reached your left arm straight ahead, the end of the bell would rest just above your wrist—not right next to your head, but out in front.

"When you're on stage," he explained, "first, think about the *audience*. Hear the music as they hear it. Take your ears out of your own head and hang them on the edge of your bell. It's not what's in your head that matters, it's what is coming out of that bell."

He went on: "Next, think about the *composer*. Ask yourself: 'Am I being a good steward of this composer's music by doing justice to the intended vision and spirit?' Only then should you think about yourself—and only insofar as you get yourself dressed and out on stage."

Audience first. Composer second. *Hang your ears on the edge of your bell.* I got it; his message was clear.

As a musician, you become audience-centric by showing up fully present and focused. Not focused on how much you've prepared or how brilliantly you're going to play or how many accolades you're going to get from your fans or your professor—but on delivering the *greatest possible impact* to everyone who paid the price of admission.

Similarly, if you want to succeed as a financial advisor, you need a truly client-centered, impact-driven focus—not a transactional approach aimed at enriching or promoting yourself.

Let's talk about the concept of *drive*. First, we'll explore how to measure your own success based on client impact and why focusing on your clients' financial well-being is most important.

Next, we'll talk about how to become *independently driven* to achieve your *own* professional goals rather than being driven purely by income. Both personal career goals and financial gain are important, and both begin with getting out of your own head and shifting your focus from sales to client impact.

There's an art and a science to this business. The art is being able to envision and communicate the greatest potential of where a client can land, by zooming out to ask the right questions and then zooming back in to paint a fuller picture of their ideal financial future.

The science involves designing an integrated, comprehensive approach targeted to each client's unique set of goals and circumstances. What do they need to do each month to achieve their goals? This approach also applies to your own career—figuring out the metrics of what you need to do each day or each week to make sure *you* get where you want to be.

You do this through unlocking your own potential to optimize client success. Not (necessarily) to beat your competition, or achieve job security, or line your own pockets. Don't get me wrong—those are great things to do. But they shouldn't be your primary focus; they should be the outcome of your primary focus.

The good news is that, whether you're driven primarily by personal goals or directly by impact, a client-centered approach will get you where you want to go. It becomes exponentially easier to earn and rise in our field when you pay attention to what matters to other people.

Ripple Effects

The art of this business requires vision, people skills, and client advocacy, in addition to expertise. What is the greatest possible positive impact you can imagine for each client's life? To answer that question, you need an in-depth understanding of not just their balance sheet but also their personal goals, family situation, attitude toward risk, and more.

To get this information, you have to build trust. First, ask the right questions and actually *listen*, then use what you learn to build the best, most comprehensive plan appropriate to each client's unique situation.

You can't authentically and consistently do that if you're distracted by how your quarterly sales record compares to that of your peers and how quickly you need the client to make a decision for your own metrics.

If you are overly focused on yourself, your advice to a client might end up being more about making *you* money or improving your own status than about what's in the best interest of the client. If a client implements your plan, and it leaves them under-prepared—because you were in a rush or needed a win—what will be the ripple effects?

What is the cost of each oversight or missed opportunity—for them and for you, for your firm and your community?

Here's one example. Several years ago, back when we still visited people in their homes, I sat down with a retirement-aged gentleman. He was, let's say, "traditional." Despite the fact that his wife of forty-plus years was home, and even in the next room, he didn't invite her to join us, preferring to meet with me alone.

The man opened by asking if I could beat his advisor's returns. I knew he had only a single life pension and no long-term care insurance for his wife. When I asked him what he ultimately wanted for himself in retirement and for his wife and adult kids as a legacy, he said he just wanted to beat his returns.

It would have been easy enough to make a character judgment, blaming this man for his lack of vision—but I didn't. I interpreted him as a good-natured, well-intentioned victim of our industry's relentless badgering about unrealized "returns" on investment statements, while mainly ignoring the actual *purpose* behind that money earned and saved: safeguarding long-term security, prosperity, and legacy for himself and his family. While this has improved over the years, we are still not connecting the dots for people like we should.

I could have convinced him that I can competitively manage a portfolio of funds. But I knew how poorly things could go if that were our only focus.

Based on the statistics (and my years of observation), it's likely this man would pass away before his spouse of four decades. At that point, his single life pension would abruptly stop, along with the lower of their two social security payments, leaving her with almost no income at all and no means of affording advanced care should she need it. Either way, her quality of life would plummet, likely forcing their adult children to adjust their lives to support the financial and health care needs of their mother.

I tried to share all of this in that meeting, but my relative inexperience could not combat the years of commercials pummeled into his head. While I don't know how things turned out for this family, this interaction haunts me each time I encounter clients whose lives get upended by a perfectly avoidable lack of planning. One that's actively *encouraged* by the traditional, shark-like, returns-focused style of financial advice.

What's Your Core Drive?

I'm not here to tell anyone what their central motivation in life or work is or should be. But if client success means nothing to you and personal gain is your only professional drive or measure for success, I do have some impactful advice for you: Find another career.

Granted, if you picked up this book, you're probably interested in how we can do a better job as a profession, and I bet you bring a high degree of integrity to your work. But just to be safe, let's go ahead and make one thing clear: I am writing this book for advisors and industry leaders who want to change this industry into something truly client centered. A field genuinely dedicated to increasing financial security and prosperity for Americans, their families, and our communities.

That's not some crunchy, sentimental plea for you to go volunteer all your time in service to humanity. You very much can—and absolutely *should*—build a successful, lucrative career for yourself through client-centered financial guidance.

Of course, there's a time and a place for volunteering. (As we'll see in part three, it's a vital and rewarding part of any advisor's outreach strategy.) But my career wasn't built on pro bono impulses. It was based on doing what I understand to be my job: to diagnose how I can have the greatest positive effect, to inform each client of that vision, and then to let them make the call.

This approach has paid off in dividends for me, my clients, and my firm. When you take extra time and care to create a comprehensive, customized financial plan, you do tend to make bigger sales over the long run. Spending more time with each client rather than most of your time canvassing for clients, means you enjoy far more wins than losses—along with genuine appreciation from clients, colleagues and community members. This, in turn, helps improve retention of both advisors and clients and builds a robust, deep-seeded referral-based business.

When people get results, they trust you. They recommend you to their loved ones. They stick around.

Our profession may revolve around money and numbers, but it is ultimately based on relationships with human beings. We are helping people make foundational decisions about their lives, legacies, and loved ones.

These lifelong client relationships grow into expansive networks of friends, family, and associates they've sent your way. This helps explain why so many successful advisors stay in the business far beyond age sixty-five. Not because they are not financially ready to retire but because when you've built a strong community network that relies on you, you don't want to leave. Not to mention, adding value to meaningful relationships becomes its own reward.

In this way, the advisors and industry leaders who succeed over the long haul have far more in common with family physicians than with Wall Street sharks.

Fist Pump versus Fist Bump

Imagine seeing a client leave the conference room, shake hands with their financial advisor, and then head to the elevator with a bit of a lift in their step. As soon as the elevator doors close, the advisor pumps their fists like they scored the game-winning goal.

The optimist in me would hope this advisor is celebrating because they just helped a client. They took the time to deeply understand the client's situation and recommend opportunities they believe will improve the client's financial future as comprehensively as possible.

That would be something worth celebrating. But in that case, why not celebrate together with the client? Why not a high five or fist bump celebrating the team rather than an out-of-sight fist pump in the air?

More likely, the advisor is celebrating what he perceives to be his own personal success at that moment. He may even be blind to the fact that there's a lot more that he could have done to help the client. (Besides, imagine how mortified the advisor would feel if the client realized they'd forgotten something and turned around just in time to witness this exuberant solo fist pump.)

Let's say that this client came in after a recent career change, and the advisor succeeded in rolling over the modest 401(k) from the client's last job into a managed retirement portfolio. If you want to look at this from a sales point of view alone, then by all means, *cha-ching!* Congratulations—you can close a deal. (One the client already knew they wanted.) But to celebrate this win with the client, with integrity, it has to feel to everyone like a mutual success. Not about scoring a sale but about celebrating clear value added by bringing something to the table that will impact the client's financial future in a meaningful way.

A traditional, *transactional* advisor would take the client's data and build up impressive pie graphs and spreadsheets to show them how the IRA they manage will outperform the 401(k). Does this positively impact the client? I would say, 90-something percent of the time, *yes*.

Are there also *other* opportunities that could have an even greater compound impact, for both the client and the advisor? One hundred percent of the time, yes.

There's nothing inherently wrong with giving the client exactly what they walked in the door asking for, but we advisors have a much greater responsibility than that. To me, the inability to see (and communicate) that fact amounts to a level of willful blindness, which we also need to take responsibility for.

I believe we have the opportunity to take one moment in time, when a client is willing to think and talk about their future, and broaden the lens. To help them see their greater financial context, identify their goals, and develop a comprehensive plan for achieving their highest financial potential. Not to upsell at every turn but to customize and communicate a long-term, comprehensive recommendation—even if that just means taking the time to build trust, walk them through some possible strategies, and plant some seeds of thought. Most people don't spend much time thinking about future financial risks, so the fleeting opportunities we get to help them focus on the future are invaluable.

As a brand-new advisor, it's natural to start out making smaller transactions involving more modest-income households. Even then, your job is not simply to close deals by delivering on client requests. If the person in front of you wants the IRA, it's fine to do your analysis and give them what they asked for. But if that's all you do, you've missed opportunities to have the most positive impact possible on clients and their families—and you may have unknowingly introduced risks.

When a client who trusts you leaves that conference room, they want to believe they're "all set." If another financial advisor approaches them, in many cases they'll decline because, in their mind, they've already worked things out with you.

In training advisors over the years, I often get asked how we can help someone who already has an advisor. My simple answer may sound a bit exaggerated, but sadly it is also true a majority of the time: "No problem, we'll just take care of the 90 percent of the job that has been left undone."

It's your responsibility to make sure your clients know *exactly* what "all set" should look like. When having a conversation with a client about their financial risks and opportunities, they don't want you in a rush to close a sale and get on to the next person. They certainly don't want you fist pumping the air as soon as their backs are turned. They want you to take personal accountability and ownership of the great responsibility you've been entrusted with.

To me, if you can't celebrate a win *with* your clients, that doesn't necessarily mean you have caused immediate harm. It just suggests there's more you could have done to help. And that is serious business.

From Sales to Impact

For many sales jobs, the products are pretty interchangeable, even for something as personal as . . . wedding bouquets. Now, I enjoy flowers as much as the next girl, but I'm not particular or sentimental about them. When I planned my wedding, I completely forgot about floral arrangements—until about four weeks before the date. (Some of you may be raising your eyebrows, but if you knew me, you'd know this type of cosmetic detail is just not my thing.)

By then, it was impossible to find a florist not already booked for another wedding that same day—so I asked, "Can you make nine more of whatever you're making for the other wedding?"

"Sure thing!" they said.

Everyone laughs when I tell this story, but I've never seen ugly wedding flowers. I just needed some beautiful, festive arrangements, and I got them—by thinking outside of the box (when the florists couldn't).

Financial planning, of course, is much more consequential. Our financial choices have enormous effects on our lives and those of our loved ones. No one's ever walked into a meeting with a financial planner and said, "Just give me exactly what you gave the last person so I can check this off my list."

These things we do—whether setting up a managed fund for retirement saving, locking in the most comprehensive insurance solutions, or helping clients commit to a savings goal—it's all deeply consequential, deeply personal stuff that people tend to dread and put off. It often feels too complicated or risky, even morbid, as in the case of life insurance.

Still, the impact of actions and inactions—whether positive or negative—will compound for years, decades, and even generations to come. Our clients need to trust that we can help them get these future-focused things in order, correctly, so they can focus on enjoying the present.

A traditional sales approach works like this: The advisor gets excited about a new product or service, then promotes the benefits and features of the product to convince the consumer it's right for them. It may be 100 percent true that the product is a good fit—to address one particular issue. But we let our clients down when we fail to also provide the fuller context of what's possible—or (sometimes even worse) when we provide the right solution in the wrong order.

For example, I have seen multiple clients with loans on their 401(k)s. It may seem like a great feature to be able to borrow against retirement savings—say to buy your first home—but having to use that feature suggests that you've probably planned out of order. A retirement account's first and best use is to build for retirement. The best place to save for a near-term purchase like a home would be a conservative taxable investment account, or simply a savings account.

For an *impact-driven* response, the advisor first figures out how the consumer's optimal financial structure would look. Because this likely requires a much more dramatic change for the client, it's next time to educate and motivate them to make the changes to implement the strategies and products that get them to this optimal result. To help them prepare for all the twists and turns that life is likely to throw their way.

Believe it or not, there are a finite number of solutions we can offer, and most of them do require a financial product to implement. Each product within this finite number of solutions was designed to offer a particular competitive advantage, something it does better than alternative solutions. While, in my opinion, there aren't many truly "bad" products, some are better suited to certain individual circumstances. It is our responsibility to correctly match these solutions to individual clients and to do so in the right order.

Of course, every client has the right to say, "No thank you. That's not my priority. Please just help me with this one thing." And that's okay. You're not paid to make people's choices for them. You are paid to provide the context needed to help clients make the best possible choices. We're here to embark on a journey with our clients, not simply to close a transaction.

What's not okay is taking an order, ignoring the responsibility you have to complete the job, and shutting the door (fist pumping) without doing your best to educate and empower them on how much more you can do for them. Instead, you've perpetuated a false belief that they've taken care of everything, which may cause harm over the long run.

Everyone has a plan, whether through deliberate choice or by passive default. If your client doesn't yet have a clear sense of their plan, they're at the mercy of whatever default results will play out if you don't interfere—and, in most cases, those results will be far from optimal.

Financial security and prosperity look different for each person and each family. Unlike wedding flowers, what we're selling should last a lifetime—and then some. That's why our advice and expertise is so valuable, as long as we evolve past the transaction-only model.

Take the time and care to really connect. Ask questions. Paint a picture of where your clients can be in the future. The choice to act or not act is theirs to make.

Own Your Confidence and Expertise

The sad thing about the hypothetical situation with the young, fist-pumping advisor is that this type of behavior—hyper-fixating on closing one narrow transaction, then chalking that up to a personal "win"—often just results from inexperience and lack of confidence.

An advisor trained from the start to think and act in a truly client-centered way—to hang their ears on the end of the bell—would approach any meeting with any client at any income level the same way. First, they would gather as much information as they could, then they would zoom out and show the client the whole picture, along with integrated, strategic short- and long-term recommendations.

Finally, they would step back and let the client decide on their ideal timing for the next steps and final outcomes. Again, this is not about pressuring clients to follow our advice but rather about making sure they have all the right recommendations—plus relevant facts, figures, and clear reasoning—to make the choices best suited for them. Ideally, they would feel empowered to take action because they now believe they can achieve better results than they'd thought possible prior to meeting you.

If instead all you do is simply deliver on client requests, you're just a retail salesperson. You become an advisor when you say, "I can absolutely help you with that. First, I'd like to take a step back and tell you more about the scope of the work we do and what I believe is possible for you." In other words, you usually have to introduce something new.

To do that, you have to own your confidence. If you're in an advisor role, it's because you have the information and solutions to guide clients toward the best possible future. Whether you know the answers from experience or because the answers and resources are at your fingertips within your firm, don't be afraid to be the guide you were hired to be.

Imagine you're a real estate agent and a couple comes in looking to buy a house. Would you just show them photographs of three houses and ask, "Which one do you want?" Of course not! You would ask questions: "Where do you work? How many bedrooms do you need? What school district are you interested in?" Then, you would use your expertise to find them their dream home, within those parameters.

You are the expert here, and it's your job to share that expertise: the process, metrics, and steps for how to get to their optimal financial future. This is part of the *science* of the business.

After you've laid out your full recommendations, the ball's in the client's court. Give them information. Then give them time, trust, and respect. The decision is theirs to make; it's their money and their life. But if you don't at least give them the options and information to make an educated decision, you're not doing your job. In fact, in *not* presenting the fuller picture, you are making a choice for them that is not yours to make.

New advisors sometimes resist recommending more thorough, comprehensive plans. This may reflect a misalignment in their core drive. Usually it's because they think their job is to sell quickly and often, but they also don't want to damage a budding relationship by "trying to upsell" too early or too quickly.

If you can truly cultivate a client-centered approach, the only reason to ever suggest or implement any of these comprehensive strategies is to optimize the client's financial future. The byproduct of that, of course, is that both the advisor and firm would also get paid. Thinking this way will make you successful, but it takes work, trust, and maturity because it's predicated on truly helping your clients succeed.

Becoming Independently Driven

So far, we've talked mainly about the art of becoming a more impact-driven financial advisor: learning to envision where a client can optimally land by zooming out to paint a fuller picture of the client's financial future, then zooming back in to take them through it one step at a time.

We also talked a little about the science of designing an integrated, comprehensive approach to getting there, targeted to each client's unique set of goals and circumstances.

Now it's time to turn both the wide-angle lens and the methodical follow-through back on yourself. If you believe that your job is to help a client achieve as much as they possibly can, you should practice what you preach.

First, partake in the art of envisioning your potential. What is the most complete picture of where *you* want to go? What is the most you can possibly achieve? Where are you headed? If you leave your house on a drive but did not decide where you were going, you may eventually find yourself right back where you started. We see this in the careers of advisors jumping from firm to firm, hoping that some external resource or context will suddenly move the needle for them.

Once you are clear on your destination, figure out your roadmap for getting there. What are the metrics for your success? What do you need to do each day or each week to make sure that you get there? When you get that right, you will have no fear of running out of clients, and you will have clear mile markers to help you find your way.

These days, after seventeen-plus years in the business, if someone makes an appointment with me, they become a client more than 90 percent of the time. But it wasn't always that way.

When I started out in this business, I was a single mom with a two-year-old boy, my entire family still lived in Canada, and all my friends were recent graduates trying to get started on their music careers. I did not come from the traditional sales, management, or finance background, and I didn't have much outside material support.

It felt like every meeting with a potential client and every potential sale carried *so much* weight. I was overly concerned about outcomes, mostly related to *myself* and what might happen to my son and me if I didn't hit my targets. When you operate out of this fear and lack-based mentality, I assure you that clients can sense it.

In this business, you must become both confident and independently driven to achieve your potential—defined not by getting your prize as quickly as possible but by adding value and having the best possible impact on your clients.

This requires a process-driven approach to personal goal setting. Because I'm process driven by nature, when a void in leadership meant I didn't get the training I needed, I created a process for both training myself and setting metrics to achieve my goals.

Now, as a leader, it's my job to help advisors become independently driven to achieve their own potential. Because when they figure out the path—*their* path—they don't need me to tell them what to do every day. They start running so fast, I can't keep up.

Probable—or Certain?

I remember early on when a business coach, Steve D'Annunzio (CEO of Mission Driven Advisor), addressed my team of fellow advisors and me.

"Raise your hand if you think it's *possible* to hit your goals for the year," he said. All hands went up.

"Keep them up if you think it's *probable*." A few hands dropped (apparently those whose strategy was "shoot for the stars.")

"Now, is it *certain* you will hit your goals?" Most hands dropped, en masse.

"Certainty" is rarely guaranteed in life, but you will get much closer if you know where you are going and have built a clear and measurable path to get there. What are your goals, and what is your fool-proof formula for consistently achieving those goals?

You may have heard of the 10-3-1 formula popular in our business for decades. The idea is that for every ten appointments you try to schedule, three people will actually meet with you, and only one of them will move forward with your advice. That math has proven pretty accurate for a very long time. It's also very transactional, focusing only on the "numbers game" without factoring in quality or acknowledging the inherent value of relationship building. I wanted an approach that focused more on adding value to people rather than reducing each of them to a number.

I decided I would aim for at least two meetings a day, four days a week, forty weeks a year. These could involve client meetings, consults, or even outreach activities to forge connections and hopefully generate introductions. The idea was not to play the numbers game needed to *close deals* for my own gain but rather to focus on adding real value to real people and growing the base of relationships that could, in turn, help me grow my business.

The first time I hit my recognition conference goals, I had locked in the science of my practice. It turns out that to guarantee the results I needed, I only had to achieve my two x four goals for eighteen out of the fifty-two weeks of each year.

After showing myself these results, my confidence soared. I now felt certain that I could achieve my initial goal. I had come up with a formula that allowed me to think about others first—about what they needed from me and how I could add value to their lives—while still considerably growing my career as a result, in a way I could measure. This also meant I was ready to set loftier goals for the next year.

Your goals and metrics may be different from mine, depending on the size of your firm, your experience and industry focus, and where you want to end up. But once you can align your internal drive away from sales and toward impact—then work out the steps for getting there—you'll be well on your way to the destination of your choosing.

Don't forget that my personal metrics had nothing to do with closing sales. I measured my progress instead in terms of human connections—genuine conversations with people. In our firm today, the metrics are different. Rather than measuring performance solely based on sales, we focus on what we call the "Core4," the four leading activities under your control, which, when perfected, result in a growing business. Sales, as a secondary measure, reflect the inevitable outcome of these activities.

Focus on these leading activities, and the proportions will naturally start to sway in your favor. Perfect these leading activities, and you will start to change lives, not the least of which will be your own.

Redefining "Wins"

Musicians who truly focus on audience impact are on a constant quest for excellence. Their performances become exercises in authentically engaging with and interpreting the artists' work, tuning into their listeners' experience, and channeling both the audience's energy and the composer's intent.

When we idolize musical artists, it's not because of the car they drive or the home they live in. While awards and rankings might get some media coverage and audience attention, fans become truly devoted to art that has an impact on them. Something they can *connect* with because it speaks directly to them.

Many well-known artists have made a huge lasting impact, shaping generations to come with the legacy of their art—without ever receiving wealth or public status during their lifetimes. Fortunately, as financial advisors and leaders, we can both achieve financial success today and also have a meaningful impact on future generations. But we are unlikely to do either if we cannot connect with our audience.

As a trombone student, I was dedicated to the music but also competitive in my own right. I auditioned for university music programs, which was a grueling process. I competed for first chair, for solos, and ultimately for professional orchestras. Throughout this competitive training, I naively thought my commitment was to the music, but I hadn't yet fully centralized the audience (which may ultimately explain why I am not still a professional musician today). You can be an artist for the sake of the art or an artist for the sake of the money. There is magic in the middle, I think. I didn't figure that out as a musician, but I find it resonates with me in the business of financial guidance in a very meaningful way.

Advisors are similarly competitive. We want high-caliber outcomes. But in prioritizing the wrong outcomes and being overtly focused on our own success, we perpetuate a negative public perception—and, for some reason, we just keep doubling down.

It can be very difficult to get started in this business. When people hit that tipping point where they figure out both the art (envisioning the best outcomes for their clients and themselves) and the science (the plan for getting there), that is when things really come together.

This has everything to do with your personal drive. When you meet with a potential client, start by thinking about them, where they are in their lives, and why they are meeting with you. Then, remind yourself: "I'm here to add value." There are many ways to add value for a client and many ways to gain value from a client. In some instances, you will be able to immediately add value and transact. In others, you will help clients set themselves up for a future time when they may need you. Maybe they don't purchase anything right away, but they do feel you're worth referring a friend to, or they simply leave feeling confident that they've found their future advisor—when they're ready. The Business Networking International (BNI) motto, "Givers gain," is founded in that very concept.

Adding value doesn't mean giving a bunch of brochures to clients or intimidating them with your industry jargon (those things are actually about you), but rather getting to know who they are and what they want out of their lives (which is about them). Then, using your knowledge and resources, you can help them envision a prosperous future, along with a strategy for getting there.

If you hear, "I'm the main breadwinner, I may have to retire by age sixty, and we have a special needs child," you should suggest something different compared to somebody who's single, has no children, and plans to work forever. Seeing TV personalities make millions providing the same cookie-cutter advice to an audience they can't see and know nothing about boggles the mind. Unless, of course, you realize that they are selling ratings, not advice. They do this by preying on their audience's fear—mainly *of us*, by the way. We have to accept and address the pure and simple fact that people turn to these sources out of fear of what will happen if they turn to us instead.

This is why it's so important for us to be willing to take the time to educate clients by caring enough to tailor a comprehensive set of personalized recommendations—all aimed at increasing positive impact, ideally for generations to come. It all starts with you prioritizing compound impact on your clients' futures, families, and communities.

Again, this is not some fluffy, idealistic manifesto for you to volunteer all your time in financial service to humanity. By having a greater positive impact on people, you will also have a greater impact on your own career. You might even end up among the roughly 15 percent of advisors who last longer than four years in our field.[5]

We can't make choices for our clients, but it is our responsibility to show them the very best they can do and educate them on how to get as close to that as possible. You can't expect to always move the needle in one conversation, but you can give them the tools and tips they need, gain their respect, and garner the value that will follow.

Finally, this is not some zero-sum game. Not only can you celebrate your colleagues' wins, but you also never have to choose between enriching yourself and enriching your clients. If you truly focus on clients and long-term sustainability as your core drive, you will find plenty of people very grateful for your help.

[5] According to a 2020 lImRa and Finseca survey: Kathleen Krozel, "A Path to Better Agent Retention.", 2022, https://insurancenewsnet.com/innarticle/a-path-to-better-agent-retention.

GUT CHECK

Are you "hanging your ears on the end of your bell"?

The next time you come out of a successful meeting, ask yourself: Can I truly celebrate this win with the client? Have I really done my best to consider and communicate the compound impact of action or inaction?

How do you measure yourself? By short-term personal gains—or a lifetime of value?

CHAPTER 2

DRIVE *for* LEADERS

A few years ago, I interviewed a young woman in her twenties for an advisor role. I'm not usually one to notice fashion details, but this woman came in wearing a Louis Vuitton bag worth more than all my bags combined. It was a notable detail for such a young person, but at the time, I rationalized it as maybe a gift from her parents.

Then we ran our customary background check. What we found were several collections accounts—including one from, yes, *Louis Vuitton*. Turns out, she'd made purchases on credit, and now collectors were coming after her for (among other things) the very bag she'd carried into an interview to become a *financial advisor*.

I'm not trying to make this into some moral failure. Maybe this individual truly believed that to break into the field of wealth management, she needed to "look the part" by *appearing* more financially successful than she was.

I understand why she arrived at that conclusion. Just look at the hiring and training norms within our field. Industry leaders traditionally recruit fiercely competitive professionals who are highly motivated by personal success. We encourage this by pitting advisors against each other, comparing their short-term sales stats, and offering trophies based on how much money they bring into the firm. Advisors even perpetuate performative spending by modeling it themselves. I've seen advisors driving cars they can't afford, buying homes they can't pay for, taking on way more debt than they need, and treating their own finances cavalierly—on the recommendation of leaders in our industry.

Shouldn't we instead measure success through impact on our clients, their families, and their communities? Shouldn't we *also* look for people driven by impact? Candidates who champion good financial health, personal responsibility, and a genuine desire to help clients thrive?

I'm not suggesting we only hire advisors who pass the *kumbaya* test. That's neither helpful nor realistic. This business is challenging and competitive. Advisors need to feel confident managing large accounts. This requires savvy, inner strength, and a strong desire to succeed. A lot of people who are primarily driven by personal success have those qualifications and will prove to be great additions to your team.

But here's the deeper industry-wide disconnect: Even those advisors motivated by money and recognition can learn to measure their professional success based on client impact. And, in fact, they should. Again, not out of some moral imperative of selflessness. Rather, because focusing on client impact is the best way to achieve personal success in this field. If you have a greater impact on clients, you genuinely earn their trust. Then, they're more likely to implement your recommendations.

They're also more likely to send clients your way, which brings in even more rewards for advisors and the firm.

For financial advisors, personal success is the natural outcome of *doing your job.* And the job is to *advise.* Is there any other context (one you would feel good about) in which people giving advice are encouraged to think first and foremost about *themselves* rather than those receiving the advice?

If you're an industry leader and you're still reading this book, you likely agree that our industry has its *own* image problem—and the problem is not that our advisors appear insufficiently fashionable or prosperous. (If you don't agree, and you're still reading, thank you. Hang in there. Take a walk in my shoes for a minute.)

So now, assuming you resonate with the idea of actually *helping* your clients achieve their optimal financial future, the next question is this: How do you build an impact-driven firm?

To me, the job of a leader is to be authentically aligned with the core drive of optimizing client success for generations to come. Our motivations reflect our values. We need to examine basic integrity across recruiting, training, and development—including how we cultivate the right core drive and how to guide our advisors to become both professionally impactful and personally successful.

If we want to build a culture genuinely focused on client outcomes, we have to pay attention to who we hire, as well as how we train and motivate our advisors and leaders to become independently driven. Finally, we have to pay attention to those factors that get in the way of advisors sticking to impact-based advising.

Recruiting

We can start by recruiting people who are at least as motivated by their *impact on others* as they are by their own personal gain—let alone *image*. It's even okay for personal gain to be a strong motivator, as long as *impact* is still a real factor. That's in part because if they don't take seriously their responsibility to add value to clients, they aren't likely to personally succeed—or even last long at all—in our field.

As we'll cover next, you can accomplish a lot through training and motivation, but the raw material has to be good. People have to come to the table with the right stuff for the job. That raw material can come in all shapes, sizes, and colors—as long as it can be molded to the job of advising.

As a performing artist who's grown into an industry leader, I do encourage you to give people a shot if they come from different professional backgrounds beyond sales, finance, and athletics. We'll talk more in chapter eight ("Change for Leaders") about the benefits of recruiting a more diverse team, for both client impact and organizational success.

Until public perception begins to shift, we'll continue to attract a lot of applicants trained in highly competitive, overtly transactional fields. But even then, we can still recruit for impact. We can ask the right questions. We can frame interviews in terms of our firms' impact-driven goals and values—and explain why this approach enriches and empowers everyone involved. For example, there are athletes who show up and do what the coach asks them to do, and then there are athletes who show up two hours before practice to chase a level of performance that pushes past their personal best. These are not the same two candidates. One has the title "athlete" which makes them a popular target for recruiters in our business due to their assumed competitive nature, the other athlete is truly driven to improve and deliver the very best performance they can to the team. "Athlete" is not enough. This is also not the *only* type of driven individual with the heart, mind and spirit to excel in our profession.

Finally, we can set the right expectations and help people think differently about our line of work. I've personally interviewed hundreds of people from all kinds of different sales backgrounds. I always make a point to explain how financial guidance differs from a more traditional sales model.

When I was growing up, my parents owned a furniture store. They mounted big signs out front. They ran television and newspaper ad campaigns. They did these things to get customers in the door, but people only ever walked in because they already knew they *wanted* something: a new couch, a bed, a dining room set.

In our business, no one ever walks through our door unbidden and says, "I just really want a few more products in my closet. What's on your shelf?" In fact, they don't tend to walk through the door at all, not unless we've already connected directly with them—or someone they trust has referred them—and we've invited them in.

We invite them in because we believe we can help guide them toward a better financial future, and we do that through building a long-term relationship they may not even realize they're in the market for. This is quite different from running a retail storefront, so it's essential that your advisors understand how to operate in our professional sphere.

To my parents' credit, they instilled in me this difference. To them, their best prospects were not the people who walked into the store, but rather the ones who invited them into their homes—to see what really could be done to make a house into the home they dreamed it could be. Inevitably, and over time, that involved comprehensive home furnishing far beyond the isolated couch or chair.

Training

Training begins the first day on the job. On that day, your new advisor is the closest they'll ever be to our clients and general public. Because they haven't yet been trained, they tend to resist some notions at first, including the idea of (early and often) making the most comprehensive recommendations to clients.

Why? Because these new advisors share some of the public's misconceptions. They think that if they make a big sale, that's a win for them as the advisor—not a win for the client, which naturally makes them uncomfortable. So, while they may still suggest additional strategies or products to clients, they're thinking of these as "upsells" for themselves, not as opportunities to add lifetime value to the client. This explains why new advisors often lack the confidence to make those recommendations.

It takes framing, repetition, and consistency from leaders to adjust this view. This brings us to the topic of training for motivation and drive. New advisors enter your firm with perspectives firmly rooted in their own experiences with the financial world. Your training should expand that perspective to include—and center—what's truly possible for clients.

Advisors need to deeply understand common client behaviors and obstacles, how money moves over time, and how much of an impact they can have if clients take their advice. It's our job to show them the influence they can have—on everything from their clients' rate of savings, debt relief, and tax burdens, to protecting family security and lifestyle, to how different vehicles impact investment efficiency.

Any one company stock will perform the same whether your client owns it or someone else does. Our value lies not in merely assessing what clients own, but rather in asking questions like these: What choices did you have to make along the way to get there? What can we do now to make the future even better?

Our profession traditionally focuses on silos and sales quotas—putting down one strategy in order to elevate another—when it may well be that our clients need multiple strategies at once. If we earn the right to be their trusted advisor, these strategies can be additive rather than combative.

Most of our advisors have been trained by leaders who share this highly limiting and counter-productive perspective. Therefore, they may grasp the *concept* of client-centered, comprehensive financial guidance, but they're wholly unprepared to think in terms of compound impact and truly see what's possible. Advisors can't guide clients toward a future they can't envision.

We need to break this outdated mold and help our advisors "unlearn" these old habits. It is our job as leaders to go far beyond what they could achieve without us in their lives and help their clients do the same.

The Spectrum of Motivation

Earlier, I talked about two main types of personal drive: those driven by personal gain and those driven by impact on others. I don't see this as some polarized dichotomy but rather as a spectrum.

I'm also not suggesting we only hire from one side of that spectrum. If diversity is truly an asset, we need the energy and mindset of fierce competitors driven by personal success at least as much as we need the mission-oriented advisors with a passion for building client relationships. Luckily, focusing on client impact will help advisors on both ends of the spectrum achieve their goals. I am suggesting that we should work to understand the core drive and values of our advisors and customize our approach of how we motivate them along the way.

If you're truly mission driven, client impact will be a more powerful direct motivator than personal gain. However, if you have *no* drive toward personal gain, your mindset may indeed be more suited to either a non-profit or volunteer context—at least one without a central, overt focus on tracking metrics and promoting fiscal growth. If a person truly thinks money is inherently evil or can't stomach a spreadsheet, they're not likely to enter our field either. The job of an advisor is to grow people's money and to keep damn good track of it all. Money has to be *important* to you if you're interested in working with it.

Alternatively, we don't want our advisors crunching every last number and obsessively tracking returns—but never drawing the connection to the positive ripple effect their efforts can have on client and community wellbeing. Our plans are not abstractions; they are living, breathing solutions that have an enormous impact on people.

Being genuinely motivated by money and recognition doesn't automatically translate to being a bad person or a bad advisor. Personally, I think we *do* want to hire people like that. And we want them to be honest and unabashed about what primarily motivates them. That way, we can help them see that the impact they have on a client's financial life will have a direct multiplying effect for them, as advisors, as well.

Again, by framing our training around this core value of client impact, we can help everyone connect the dots. We need to integrate impact into everything we do. We can do that by showing metrics that support those connections: between making sales and adding client value, between earning as an advisor and adding client value, between advancing to a leadership position and—yes—adding client value.

It all comes down to impact. Compound impact.

What Motivates You?

So far, we've talked about core drive—whether that's helping others or personal gain (and how either drive can be tied directly to client impact).

This is a little different from ongoing support and morale building, so, next, let's talk about how to motivate advisors to achieve their potential. What helps people stay energized and engaged from day to day, week to week, and year to year?

Think of core drive as the direction you're going in and motivation as the fuel for getting there.

When you start asking people what they do to motivate themselves, you'll hear about vision boards, business plans, or games people play with themselves involving personal rewards. I have one advisor who loves sailing. One of his first goals was to earn enough to buy a sailboat, which he later traded up for a faster one he could use in races.

When I first started out, my personal motivation was strong. I needed to build this career to take care of my son and our home. Although I desperately wanted to succeed, I would too often finish the day or week without hitting my goals. This led to cycles of stress, self-doubt, and fear of failure.

Eventually, I decided to take the pressure off by focusing on a simple reward rather than focusing on what might happen if I failed. I used to walk past a bakery every day on my way to work, and the fresh baked bread smelled like heaven. So, after committing to my process of two meetings a day, four days a week, that was how I would reward myself. Every week that I achieved that goal, I'd buy myself a heavenly, still-warm, fresh-baked loaf on my way home. Simple and, yes, surprisingly effective.

It doesn't matter what the particular motivational tool is as long as it does the trick of getting your advisors in front of enough people. The thing about cultivating a truly impact-driven culture is that it only works when your advisors have enough clients to see. Otherwise, the fear and lack begin to creep in, along with those dollar signs on their foreheads.

Say a client comes in without savings or any semblance of a plan—and she has considerable debt besides. As an advisor without enough clients to see, I might be thinking, *I need this client to take action right away because I need to get paid.*

However, if I were an advisor twenty years in the business with a robust client network, I would instead say, "I really want to see you investing and protecting your future. But my first priority is getting you foundationally in good shape and in a position to start protecting and building real and lasting wealth." Whether or not this individual can be a client today is not the point. The point is whether or not I can help them become a great client in the future.

Having personalized metrics, like my two x four x forty strategy, helped me ensure that I would meet my goals. Not that it was *possible*, or just *probable*—but actually *certain.* In fact, I only needed to hit my two-meetings-four-days-a-week goal for eighteen weeks—less than half of my original goal of forty weeks. Seeing things this way helped me relax and better focus on the best interests of my clients. The Core4 structure we have today reflects a more evolved version of that original plan, measuring new client meetings, as well as introductions, new relationships, and centers of influence.

Financial advisors cannot afford to be professional volunteers. When we start struggling financially ourselves, it becomes very difficult to avoid becoming jaded and falling into a bad transaction cycle of pushing products to survive and compete. We should aim to achieve a balance—a culture that empowers advisors to excel and succeed, while simultaneously having the maximum impact on their clients' lives. What drives and motivates each advisor will be different, and it's our job to tie all of it back to client success. This requires discipline, rooted in the commitment to a better future, as well as a modicum of patience.

Different people respond to different things, but we can all be molded to some extent. Generally speaking, parents will fiercely advocate for their children, even those who were pretty myopic before they had kids. Why? Because they've become emotionally connected to and invested in their kids. With consistent training, we can help most advisors to also become more personally, *genuinely* invested in the success of their clients. (And if they turn out to be hopeless narcissists, we can urge them toward a new career.)

As leaders, it's on us to help advisors evaluate and honestly identify their individual core drive—not to give us the answer they think we want to hear.

It's on us to help them leverage their day-to-day motivators to become independently driven so they can fulfill their own potential and achieve success—with integrity.

Finally, it's on us to connect both their core drive and their personal motivators back to the central aim of optimizing client impact.

Integrity Check

Several years ago, I attended a session with Ed Ayala, the current CEO of Ayala Coaching Experience. He asked all the advisors in the room to take out a piece of paper and fold it in half. Next, he told us to write on one half of the paper what we do for a living. On the other half of the paper, he asked us to write down what we *told clients* we do for a living.

It was jarring to realize how many people—the handy majority—had two different things written down. What they'd been telling *themselves* they do for a living turned out to be substantially different than what they'd been telling their clients.

From my seventeen years in the business, I'd say that, most of the time, there's no intent from the advisor to dupe their client. They just happen to buy into the same public perception that's been harming our client base.

Advisors tend to come into the business thinking that they're *supposed* to be saying something different. Mainly because they haven't yet internalized the fact that optimal client success is inextricably linked to optimal advisor success. That product sales, when recommended in good faith, can and should be celebrated as a mutual win *with* the client.

This integrity check extends to leaders as much as to advisors. I've seen impact-driven advisors dedicated to the relationships they build—who abruptly shift once they become leaders. Suddenly, everything shifts to bringing in sales for the good of the *bottom line* because they have a new role and a new type of pressure. They start recruiting for volume, knowing full well that some candidates they've targeted are not the right fit.

What we say behind closed doors, how we think about ourselves, how we recruit and train our advisors—it all matters. I strongly believe that optimizing client impact will grow everyone's business and everyone's market share, but only if our investment in our clients' success is genuine.

If we can help advisors see how helping clients helps companies, then people will adjust their lens automatically. We may still recognize or reward advisors for assets under management (AUM)—especially those primarily motivated by personal gain and recognition. But why not also track, recognize, and reward *client-centered* metrics, such as the number of families or individuals helped in a certain period of time, the increase in clients' rate of savings, or the amount of protection in place for client assets?

For me, these impact-driven figures control the long-term financial success of a firm much more than what the company earns off of products in a particular quarter, or the growth of AUM between January 1 and December 31 of a single year. When playing games to land on the top of a leaderboard by the end of the year, it's important to ask yourself: Who am I really doing this for? Who benefits the most? Is there a net value or net cost to the organization?

I am not saying you shouldn't try to cross the finish line first, but I am suggesting you think deeply about what you are doing to get there and why.

Customize Your Leadership

If you're an advisor worth your salt, you already know how to take a customized approach when advising your clients. Once you're a leader, it's time to apply those strengths to training and motivating your team.

Your job as a leader is to help people, wherever they fall on the spectrum of personal drive, find their way to that maximum impact—which will also result in their maximum success.

Personally, I'm not motivated by rankings or prizes or fierce competition. If you ask me to compete with somebody, I'm more likely to say, "Let's cross the finish line together," or I'll focus on beating my personal best. I want to improve, but for me to do that, it is not necessary for someone else to lose.

I still need to recognize and appeal to different drives and motivating factors among my team. I believe that by being honest with ourselves about our motivations, we can leverage them into leadership strengths. Maybe I personally don't care about trophies, but if half the organization does, how can I run a firm effectively without recognition programs?

Leaders have to be able to guide advisors (and other leaders) who are completely different from them. We can't just clone ourselves to fill the ranks, and we wouldn't want to anyway. Echo chambers and yes-people doom companies and fail to effectively mirror their communities.

If we hold everyone to our own rigid notion of how to be effective, we're also more likely to micromanage, overcorrect, and handhold. This prevents our advisors from developing the autonomy needed to thrive and has a measurable impact on scalability.

The best version of me will be the best version of *me*. It won't be the second-best version of you. That formula of what motivates people, what clicks with them, what helps them be crystal clear about where they're headed and how they're going to get there—it's your job as a leader to help advisors peel back the layers and find that gold.

Get to know your advisors like you'd get to know your clients. You do this by asking the right questions, listening to the answers, and paying attention to the results your leadership gets.

Finally, you need to know when it's time to adjust your approach. If you keep pushing the same morale builders, and you're getting the same sub-par results, it's time to try something different.

Too many leaders remain unaware of their own blinders. They'll give the same advice over and over without paying attention to the results. Recognize whether or not you're having an impact as a leader and know when to take personal accountability and find a new approach. Your advice and techniques may have worked for you, but that doesn't mean they'll work for everyone. Not everybody thinks the way you do and not everybody is motivated by the same things.

Put your script aside and start to pay attention to the people around you. Measure your impact. Evaluate your approach. Hang your ears on the end of your bell when it comes to leadership too.

Sometimes, that means avoiding shortcuts, especially the shortcut of stepping in too fast when an advisor struggles. As leaders, we've all fallen into the trap of swooping in when an advisor's in trouble, taking over the client, closing the case, and getting results. It's easier and faster than teaching them. We tend to chalk that up to a win, when, in fact, it's a huge loss—for our clients and for the advisor. Because, in bailing our advisors out, we fail to train or empower them moving forward.

Finally, while competitiveness can be a great leadership strength, competing with your advisors is decidedly not. Each member of your team can and should become so independently driven that they end up excelling far beyond where you could get them. It is your job to buoy them up, not to hold them down.

This is my counterargument to author John Maxwell's leadership maxim, "The Law of the Lid." Maxwell states that a person's level of effectiveness remains capped by leadership ability. I agree with the concept, but I would add that with truly effective leadership, advisors will grow beyond you. Once they unlock their own formula for becoming self-motivated and independently driven, your advisors should fly toward fulfilling—even exceeding—their potential.

Finally, a note for leaders of leaders. Your leaders should similarly grow to the point where they have complete ownership over their roles and responsibilities, all focused on impact and outcomes. It's just one more layer of the same thing. Don't be afraid to let them be smarter, faster, and more effective than you are—what a win for the organization if they are!

Help each individual figure out where they fall on that spectrum between personal gain and helping others. Guide them toward devising their own motivational strategy to keep them going every day and guarantee their success. Drive them toward those points of recognition that result in maximum impact—for the leader, for the advisor, and for the client.

First, we do that through skillful recruiting. The Louis Vuitton-toting candidate going into unnecessary debt to *appear* successful at a job interview may seem ironic or even comical, but it reflects a very real misalignment within our field. For any leader in the business looking to create an impact-driven practice, it's also a red flag.

It's okay to hire competitive individuals motivated by personal gain, as long as they *also* genuinely care about adding value through long-term client relationships aimed at optimizing client impact.

Next, we reinforce this drive through proper training and motivation. We help advisors and leaders alike to understand their core drive, plus introduce those day-to-day morale boosters that will keep them going strong.

Finally, we empower them toward greater autonomy so they truly own their own client relationships, goals, metrics, and processes.

Point them in the right direction (drive), then help them fuel their own path toward success (motivation).

By now, we've established that client impact directly promotes the success of advisors and leaders alike. Whether they're motivated by recognition/wealth or directly by impact, we want them to do all they can to best help their clients—because that benefits everyone.

Now, how do we help the *general public*—our new and prospective clients—understand that same idea? Given the public image of our field, how do we correct the general misconception that we're trying to sell them products *not* to optimize their financial futures but instead to line our own pockets at their expense?

We do that by building trust.

GUT CHECK

What motivates you more: competition and personal gain—or the impact of your work on others' lives?

Are you focused on what will motivate you to get to your activity goals each week, or are you accepting lackluster results?

What do you do for a living? What do you tell your clients you do for a living?

For leaders: What do you do for a living, and what do you tell your advisors you do?

CHAPTER 3

TRUST *for* ADVISORS

A few years back, I (very briefly) advised a couple of young professionals living with their two children in the greater New York metropolitan area. Let's call them Melissa and Theo. Their combined household income of $200,000 was perfectly sufficient for raising kids, owning a home, and saving money for extras like vacations. When they came to me, Theo voiced frustration with their lack of savings. Like many, they'd tried setting a budget and sticking to it—and they were failing miserably.

After reviewing their situation, I began by pointing out that the biggest risk to their family would be if something happened to their ability to earn. I advised them to first secure disability and life insurance plans to protect the family income stream, and then to focus on saving.

The couple resisted, expressing a severe lack of trust in the insurance industry. This lack of trust could result from an experience with a pushy salesperson, a bias passed down from older generations, fear that the insurance company wouldn't fulfill its promises, or a handful of other reasons. While I did manage to convince Theo to put some insurance in place, Melissa flat-out refused, stating she'd rather focus on saving. I helped them put together a savings plan, but, unfortunately, they continued to take money out as quickly as they put it in.

Without any significant insurance, savings, or investments for me to help them manage, this couple fell off my radar—until a couple of years later, when I got a call from Melissa.

"Amy, you said that if we worked with you for a few years, we'd be able to borrow against our accounts," she said, explaining that she wanted to conjure up about $20,000—for something that most would agree was certainly not necessary and that they certainly hadn't financially planned for. Unfortunately, because they hadn't trusted me enough to take my advice, they didn't have either investment accounts or adequate insurance policies to borrow against.

I'm not sure if Melissa managed to get a loan, but about a year after that, I got another call from her—asking for my opinion on the crowdfunding platform, GoFundMe.

This time, she was raising money for a different surgery—one that was vitally necessary. Melissa had become ill, and she couldn't return to work.

The disability insurance I'd suggested just a few years earlier would have cost this couple about $50 a month. It would have replaced her full income as long as she needed it, which in this case would have generated about a half a million dollars for the family over the years she was unable to work.

You can easily imagine the ripple effects for families who find themselves in this type of situation. Downsizing to a smaller home in a less expensive school district. Sacrificing extracurriculars, summer camps, potential college savings. Taking on heavy medical debt for years to come.

In 2024, there are some 200,000 GoFundMe accounts set up to help pay medical expenses and another 125,000 for funeral expenses.

More often than not, when a client chooses not to follow through on our advice, it comes down to a lack of trust. If they were not referred to us by someone they know well and whose advice they respect, we face a heavier lift in terms of establishing trust. It could be that very few (if anyone) among their circle of family and friends have worked with a financial advisor. When clients have limited and/or negative experiences with financial advising, the mountain of reasons they mistrust the financial industry can prove too big to climb in one consultation meeting alone.

Regardless of their reasons, Melissa and Theo chose not to act on my advice. For me as an advisor, the negative impact was minimal—I was out maybe a few hundred dollars. But as you can see, the impact of failing to establish trust can be devastating to the very people who most need our help.

We can only protect our clients and grow their assets if we first *build trust*. Until we can repair what's broken in our industry, it's the everyday people like Melissa and Theo who suffer most from the lack of public trust in what we do. Not the advisors, media outlets, or government entities. Not the wealthier clients, who tend to have more familiarity with financial strategies and are generally quicker to act.

Unfortunately, this story is all too common. Many average Americans learn from uneducated, unlicensed "expert" personalities with broad appeal to mistrust our profession. But we are partly responsible for that lack of trust.

And we are 100 percent responsible for rebuilding it.

We need to educate our lawmakers to ensure that regulations put in place *help* rather than harm and (ideally) hold influencers without licenses accountable for their antics. Most importantly, we have to do a better job of explaining to our prospective clients the importance of getting advice tailored specifically to them.

We can only rebuild trust through others-focused, impact-driven financial guidance—by hanging our ears on the bell, which, in our case, requires skillful listening, meeting clients where they are, and empowering them to take full command over their financial futures.

Regulation

First, a brief word on the impact of government regulations on our industry and how that's commonly viewed. As I see it, all of these entities are trying to regulate trust, whether it's the Department of Labor (DOL), the Security and Exchange Commission (SEC), the Financial Industry Regulatory Authority (FINRA), or a state insurance regulator. And they do that by restricting how we do our jobs.

Unfortunately, their "solutions" tend to breed more fear than trust. One recent example relates to the DOL's fiduciary rule. The rule requires advisors to work completely void of conflicts of interest. Which sounds great on the surface, but it is completely impossible and does not give adequate consideration to downside risk, with the effect of encouraging a limited product choice. Those distinctions are critical to the future of the profession and consumer choice.

When companies and legislators promote fiduciary advice as the only option for clients, it does more harm than good.

That's because the definition of fiduciary advice is biased toward one type of financial solution. I believe this will have the unintended consequence of both limiting consumer choice and making it more difficult to work with clients with smaller accounts.

If you pause your television during one of those fiduciary-only ads, you'll see at the bottom of the screen that to work with one of these people, clients must have a minimum level of assets—in some cases, at least $500,000. At any level of investment, this model trains entire generations of middle-class Americans to think: A. They're not safe with financial advisors unless they're licensed fiduciaries, and B. They may not actually qualify for any services. Once we are all fiduciaries all the time, we won't need these ads, but the minimums will still apply.

The legal definition of "fiduciary" is easy enough if you're buying, say, shares of Apple stock. No matter what company you buy the shares from, they're selling you the same exact Apple stock at the same exact market rates. In this situation, there aren't other things to consider aside from the two functions to an investor: value and dividends. These operate the same way regardless of where or how they're bought.

As soon as you get into the realm of insurance products, things get more complicated. For example, when it comes to guarantees for annuity products, you have to consider the strength of the individual insurance companies in addition to the clients' situations. Even if you do so through the lens of maximizing positive client impact, it now becomes necessary to consider any of these products as "prohibited transactions" and apply for an exemption to sell them. There is no way to read these regulations and not see that bias. An insurance or annuity product is designed to deliver service beyond returns. While the equity is just about return and dividend, insurance begins with a risk transfer from a client to the insurance company.

The primary reason for the high minimums at some firms is that, under a strictly fee-based model, it can be cost prohibitive for us to work with clients still building their wealth. However, this practically guarantees that those clients get deprived of professional guidance until they reach the fiduciary minimum. How much faster could clients get there with our advice and support? How many mistakes could we help them avoid along the way?

This ridiculous complexity poses a number of problems. First, firms may impose or raise asset minimums to compensate for the increased burden of disclosure. They may also limit product choices for clients with fewer assets. The people most likely to get left behind as a result are middle-class consumers—precisely the ones who most need products with some kind of guarantee and less market risk. This is especially true now that there are less than 47,000 defined benefit pension plans in the US, compared with over 175,000 in the 1980s.[6]

I genuinely believe that neither the DOL nor the companies with higher minimums intend to harm consumers. Still, the side effect of an outdated approach that pits one strategy against another is that people who need more secure strategies don't get the financial guidance they need.

[6] Employee Benefits Security Administration, US Department of Labor, "Private Pension Plan Bulletin Historical Tables and Graphs 1975-2021," September 2023, https://www.dol.gov/sites/dolgov/files/ebsa/researchers/statistics/retirement-bulletins/private-pension-plan-bulletin-historical-tables-and-graphs.pdf.

A few weeks ago, some colleagues and I went to Albany, New York, to talk to representatives about new state regulations, including Reg. 187, which (again, in theory) was designed to protect the public from all conflicts in insurance sales.

We explained to them that the year after Reg. 187 went into effect, we happened to see a national increase in the number of insurance policies sold, by about 13 percent—*except* in New York state, where insurance sales actually dropped by 5 percent. This demonstrates an 18 percent trust gap in New York, resulting in at least 55,000 fewer Americans obtaining insurance products to protect their incomes, assets, and families.

Even more frightening than this drop in applications is the fact that the net volume earned from insurance premiums (how advisors get paid) actually *increased* in New York state. Even though there were 55,000 fewer policies sold, those that were sold tended to be larger, more comprehensive plans—a clear example of the rich getting richer (better protected) and the poor getting poorer (more financially vulnerable).

Because of Reg. 187, some insurance applications in New York state increased to one hundred-plus pages of regulatory jargon and legalese. Wealthier people with advisors and more experience with complex documents remained unfazed. But average Americans—the ones who most need this kind of protection—were understandably put off by this volume of paper and questions they needed to sift through and answer just to complete a simple transaction. It would be understandable for clients to ask, "If this is good for me, why do I need to sign so many pages of disclosures?"

To see the full impact, let's go a level deeper. Who is serving these younger or more middle-class Americans? Typically, it's the newer advisors, as more experienced advisors tend to work on larger accounts with wealthier clients. Not only are the people most in need of insurance products not getting them, but they're also getting less experienced, less confident advisors (the ones more prone to burn out and drop out—especially when their clients don't trust them enough to take their advice).

This idea that you have to already be wealthy to seek personalized financial advice is one of the most common and damaging misconceptions about our field. No one would ever say, "I'm not sick enough yet to go to the doctor." We go in for regular well visits and screenings for a reason—to promote actual *health* versus only reacting defensively to illness. Encouraging Americans to wait until they have $500,000 on hand to seek financial guidance actively harms public financial health—far more than it hurts advisors.

If advisors take the responsibility to become impact driven and client centered, perhaps regulators will begin to turn their focus to improving outcomes for consumers rather than trying to regulate every interaction, and more people will get the help they need. An improved level of trust in our profession would certainly help advisors just starting out in the business, but more importantly, when you see 55,000 Americans in just one year losing financial protection (in one state alone), it's clear that the more vital metrics have to do with impact on our clients and communities.

Good First Impressions Pay Dividends

There's critically important work to be done advocating for our industry and for the American public as members of our professional associations. However, the real day-to-day progress happens when we sit down with clients, and not just in terms of educating them by demystifying complex jargon and dubious regulatory logic. To truly and efficiently add value, we must, first and foremost, listen—especially when making our first impression.

Many advisors express frustration in the results they are getting, but then they reveal that they made initial recommendations to prospective clients over an impromptu phone call or in a casual setting that's not a meeting dedicated specifically to the task. In doing so, they skip important info-gathering about a client's financial situation, values, and goals. This practice of trying to advance to the transaction erodes consumer trust and weakens your impact. There is nothing casual about people's financial futures, so make sure to treat meetings with the respect your clients deserve. When you rush to a sale, you are effectively saying, "This really isn't important."

Whenever possible, make sure there are no distractions during that all-important first meeting—for you or for your clients—and be sure to listen far more than you speak. When you do speak, you should be asking questions. This is the antithesis of the celebrity advisor or social media influencer, who only speaks and presents. That's not us. As client-centered, impact-driven advisors, our job is to make sure that *before* we give any advice, we have all the information we need to make the greatest impact.

Following these principles keeps clients with us year after year. Client retention arguably represents the most definitive sign of trust, as well as the greatest return on our investment. When clients trust you enough to stay, they will inevitably implement more strategies with you over the years, increasing their financial success—and yours right along with it. Sustained client relationships will also increase referrals, improving your bottom line even more. As you work with clients, their families, and their other professional advisors, you will effectively turn your practice into a self-sustaining ecosystem—with a moat around it.

Client-Centered Education

I've seen advisors completely dejected when a client—or sometimes a friend, neighbor, or relative—mentions having made an important financial move the advisor could have handled for them. When the advisor asks why they didn't reach out for help, the client often says, "I didn't know you did that!" Take this as valuable feedback; you clearly didn't paint the full picture if clients and close associates don't understand the scope of your work.

While we need to educate clients on all the things we do, we also need to keep the focus on them—not us. Another common mistake involves putting too much attention on yourself. Some advisors think they have to be the smartest person in the room—*that's why clients come to us for advice, right?* Nope! We don't gain trust by puffing out our chests, looking for approval. Clients are more likely to trust the advisors who make the meeting about them and their lives.

If it were true that we need to show superior intellect to impress our clients, why would a billionaire ever seek advice? Obviously, billionaires earn more than the average financial advisor, and it would be reasonable to assume they are pretty smart as well. Billionaires don't hire advisors because they lack the brainpower to make complex decisions but because they recognize that they don't have the time to research and detect all their potential opportunities and blind spots. They delegate to a team of advisors so they can spend their time elsewhere.

Other advisors end up self-interested in a paradoxical way by focusing too much on "helpfulness" and going out of their way to demonstrate that they're providing the best *service* possible. But being helpful and customer service-oriented is not the same as being *valuable*. You can be super helpful—confirming meetings, showing up early, deferring to a "customer's always right" mentality—and end up spending far too much time gaining approval without truly adding much value.

There's also a big difference between helping in the moment—selling a single life insurance policy or just setting up someone's IRA, for example—versus putting together a truly comprehensive strategy for optimal long-term success. This fragmented approach might feel like it helps your short-term sales numbers . . . but it won't have the most lasting compound impact on the client, nor will it bring the most returns to you or your firm over the long run.

Sometimes you may have an opportunity to present something in a community setting about what you do for a living. If so, resist the self-interested urge to focus on your degrees, certifications, and accolades. Instead, put your attention on metrics and messaging related to positive compound impact on clients. I recently had an advisor tell me about one such opportunity in a structured networking group she'd joined. Because of her background in acting, this creative advisor reimagined a popular sitcom to describe what she did. While I'm sure it was incredibly entertaining, this approach had the regrettable effect of putting all the attention on her, not on her client impact. This is the opposite of what we want to do. We want people to hear about what we do and leave thinking, *Wow, this advisor works with people just like me,* not *Wow, that was really entertaining.*

Always make it *genuinely* about your prospective clients. When meeting with them, ask questions. Listen to the answers. Then, ask more questions. Gather as many details as you can about their finances, goals, and potential risks and obstacles. That way, you can more efficiently and effectively tailor specific, client-focused, long-term advice.

While doing so, you'll likely uncover some biases and misconceptions, whether about specific products or the financial advising industry in general. Much of this will be rooted in misinformation your clients picked up from mainstream or social media, or even from well-meaning family and friends. How do we combat this without damaging client trust?

Misinformation

Much of our industry's poor public image comes down to simple misinformation. Complex matters get watered down into sensationalist talking points that either oversimplify or mischaracterize information, often through competing narratives.

Media outlets would rather gain clicks and viewers than do their due diligence, and the result is mass confusion. Just look at medical reporting on something as common as a morning coffee. Is coffee good for you or bad for you? It seems like the answer changes every two weeks.

When it comes to these celebrity advisors or influencers, it's important to understand what they're getting paid for—and it's not giving advice. Typically it's to book speaking engagements, increase viewership and engagement (ratings, clicks, "likes," etc.), or sell merchandise and subscriptions.

Other times, misinformation comes from friends and family recommending something in good faith—something that may have worked well for them but remains completely irrelevant to your client's unique situation.

Let's say you have a young client who just started a new job, and his newly retired Uncle Jim urged him to immediately start maximizing contributions into his 401(k). This well-meaning family member's advice is colored by the fact that, unlike his twenty-something nephew, he's just hit retirement age. The conversations in his orbit, the articles he's reading—all of it reinforces advice for retirees, which may not apply to our new prospective client.

As advisors, we appreciate the value of a well-stocked 401(k). But we also know that saving for retirement is just one piece of the puzzle—one isolated product, not a financial plan. So many things need to be accounted for between that first job and retirement: insurance products, savings accounts, student debt payments, liquid investments, and more. Meanwhile, things like tax rates and market conditions may impact the young client differently than his uncle. Our job is to find out everything we can about the client's income, spending habits, educational loans, etc., then build a comprehensive, strategic plan with the highest probability of protecting the client against variables and delivering optimal future success.

How do we combat such misinformation without turning our client against Uncle Jim—or, *way* more likely, turning them both against us?

Start by "embracing the rationale."

Embrace the Rationale

I borrow this phrase from Maria Ferrante-Schepis, co-author of *Flirting With the Uninterested: Innovating in a "Sold, Not Bought" Category*. "Embracing the rationale" means meeting clients where they are. That means digging around for the nugget of helpful intent buried within any misaligned advice. Only then can we effectively flip the script and move on to something more relevant and impactful.

In our Uncle Jim example, embracing the rationale might sound like this: "It's great you have family who care about your financial future and that you are engaging them in these conversations to get their perspective. It sounds like your uncle is in the enviable position of being able to retire after decades of hard work. We absolutely will get to the right 401(k) plan contribution for you, but first let's explore the bigger picture of your current financial health and where you want to be. Then I can guide you to the best solutions to get you there—in the right order. Don't forget that you're just starting out in your career, and your trajectory may look a bit different."

If the first thing you say is, "Your Uncle Jim doesn't know what he's talking about," you will alienate the client, confirming their likely suspicion that you're just trying to upsell them against their best interests.

You cannot create a greater degree of trust with someone you just met than they have with someone they've known their whole life. Don't try to do that. Instead, earn your way into that circle by respecting the trust your clients have for those around them. With this approach, you're far more likely to be welcomed into the fold.

This applies to the celebrity advisors, as well as the hordes of social media influencers. (To me, it's fair to lump them all together because they're all presenting generalized information to a broad audience.) If client misconceptions happen to come from someone whose books they've read or whose online content they've followed for years, they'll have a lot more exposure to—and built-in trust around—that source. Be careful also when countering information from previous advisors; we do ourselves a disservice by attacking our own industry. Whether or not we agree with all the advice that's made it to the table already, that advice has informed your client's perspective, which you need to understand before you can influence, counter, or correct anything.

Clients often tell me about some conventional "wisdom" they've heard—for example, that they're supposed to pay off their mortgage by the time they retire. Sure, that might make sense for some individuals. If you blindly throw enough darts, you'll hit the bullseye eventually. But any kind of global universal advice will be inherently wrong for most people. In some circumstances, paying off that mortgage early is exactly the right decision. However, let's say a client took out a thirty-year mortgage in 2015 at a 3 percent interest rate. If they threw all their liquid funds at this loan, they could lose valuable opportunities to pay off high-interest credit card debt, save for retirement, or invest in products that protect their financial future. After a comprehensive analysis, you can point out all the ways that such a unilateral plan might actually cost them big by forgoing the other vehicles that promote long-term financial health. (Not to mention the fact that many people sell their house and pay off the remaining mortgage when they retire anyway.)

First though, recognize the power of the influencer—whether it's a social media financial "guru" or someone's brother-in-law. Find a way to make their trusted source "right," even if only in intent. After you've affirmed the source, it's your job to bridge the gap. Help them understand why the particular piece of information they came across in their Google search or news feed may be a good point to consider but may not be the most appropriate, impactful advice for them personally at this time.

Know Your Worth

This ability to tailor advice to an individual reflects the true worth of an advisor—one who will never be replaced by one-size-fits-all advice from celebrities, influencers, or even algorithmic, direct-to-consumer robo-advisors.

When it comes to financial health—much like medical health—there's a tipping point where a consumer believes the decision is too important for them to make themselves. If you get a mild, isolated headache, you're not going to call the doctor. You'll probably just take an aspirin. But if you suddenly start getting headaches every single day, or if the pain gets intense enough, you'll eventually make an appointment to see a physician.

Now, the reason people tend to respect their doctor's advice (even when they don't want to) is because doctors enjoy more public trust than we do as financial advisors. I personally don't love finding time to fit all the standard screenings, bloodwork, and follow-ups into my schedule, but I still go to doctors and follow their advice because fundamentally I know it's good for me.

We want to try to build that trust in our industry as well. All the expertise in the world will get you nowhere without trust. On the flip side, once you do build that trust, people will understand your worth. They will recommend you to people they know, who will then walk in your door predisposed to listen to what you have to say. There's no number of credentials or letters after your name that will go as far as somebody they trust telling them, "My experience with that advisor was amazing. You should really talk to them." As you will see in the chapter on engagement, the higher the trust in the source of the referral, the more readily the new client will extend that trust to you.

Behavior Modeling

Part of your worth as an advisor involves educating and empowering your clients to make better financial decisions on their own. This happens naturally when you develop genuine, long-term relationships with clients and model good financial reasoning.

Often, after I've been working with clients for a while, they'll call me up and say, "Hey, I've decided to make this financial move." This could be anything from investing in a second home, paying off a debt, or changing an allocation in their portfolio. Whatever it is, they tend to say, "I figured the first thing you would do is ask me A, B, and C. So that's how I came to this decision. Did I get it right?"

At that point, all I have to say is, "Yes! Good thinking."

With each client, you should be able to recognize the specific order of operations that best promotes their financial health outcomes. That order of operations informs how we want clients to think about money. It's the "PEMDAS" of our profession.

We can think about trust in much the same way. We have to show our work by explaining and modeling the responsible financial behavior we want clients to adopt through lifelong relationships. Educate them to really understand the principles underlying your planning. Help them internalize that logic so they can make better choices on their own.

Take Responsibility

We can see the harm done by media propaganda and misguided government efforts to protect consumers. As advisors, we may not be responsible for the public's lack of trust in us, but it is our responsibility to repair that trust. We can't stop the misinformation or the bad actors, but we can build the trust needed to get to the best possible outcome for each individual client. And I assure you, the ripple effects are powerful.

As advisors, we could have massive potential impact if we stopped competing so hard and fighting each other. If we stood together and focused on truly educating and empowering our clients and communities.

As noted in part one, repairing public trust begins with examining our own core drive and motivations—and aligning the same drive toward maximizing positive compound impact on our clients' financial futures.

Next, we have to really listen and meet people where they are. Even when talking to Congress about regulatory issues, I start by embracing the rationale. I point out that the intent behind the fiduciary rule is noble and good: to put the client's interests first. From there, I can explain why there may be unintended consequences.

I'm certainly not saying that everyone in our field is always acting in their clients' best interests. We do need legislation that prevents bad apples from ruining the bunch—and fortunately in the majority of states we do have best-interest regulation already. The problem is that there is a true lack of understanding of the ripple effects of trying to regulate trust.

My goal is to encourage real change through impact-driven, client-centered financial guidance. Sometimes that means shining a light on the brutal impact that this lack of trust can have on real people—like the example of Melissa and Theo. That couple's lack of trust in my financial advice didn't change my life. It didn't change the lives of any elected officials or talking heads in the media. But it did harm these clients' lives and the lives of their children.

As individual advisors and leaders, there's so much we *can* do to build trust in the financial advising industry—but it's not going to happen overnight. Like most things, change starts with how we manage our own business: how we align our core drive and motivations, how we approach our clients, and how we engage in our communities.

It's on us to take responsibility and build trust. To ask questions—then really listen. To embrace the rationale behind poor advice—then bridge the gaps. Finally, to know our worth and empower our clients through building genuine relationships and behavior modeling.

GUT CHECK

Did you *really listen* today?

When confronted with a misinformed client, were you able to find a genuine way to "embrace the rationale?"

Do you consistently think beyond the transaction to the maximum potential impact and work to paint that picture?

Are you implementing your own advice and modeling good financial choices?

Are you getting consistent introductions and referrals from your clients—a demonstration of their trust in you?

CHAPTER 4

TRUST *for* LEADERS

A colleague of mine once observed that the men we were hiring tended to have more confidence than ability, while the women tended to have more ability than confidence.

This was an overly generalized observation, of course. We'd seen both men and women who defied these trends, but one main point remains: For any advisor to earn client trust, they need both confidence *and* ability.

I recently sat down with a newer advisor, a young woman who was running out of people to reach out to (an issue we'll unpack more in the next two chapters on engagement). This challenge, so common during advisors' early years, can quickly erode confidence. I have a tendency to be direct (bordering on sarcastic)—especially when I believe these young women are far more amazing than they realize—so I challenged her.

"If you open the contacts on your phone, starting with 'A,' you can tell me you've called every person in there?" She started to say "yes," but she didn't even believe it herself. I persisted, asking her to pull up the first contact on her phone. "Have you called them?" I asked.

She hadn't. That first name was her father's advisor. "If you called him right now and asked him to meet for coffee, would he agree?"

"Of course," she replied, "but I don't feel confident making the call without knowing what to say in the meeting."

I explained that confidence gets built in small wins. "Take that first step, knowing you will get a 'yes,'" I said. "Just take the meeting, then I'll help you figure out what to say."

Once she had the meeting, she came back to me for next steps. I gave her a laundry list of questions: "How did you get into the business? What are the most important lessons you learned? How did my dad become your client? When did you feel like you got your first break? How do you build your business today? What would you do differently if you were starting today? Do you know any young attorneys or accountants or other centers of influence who I might benefit from meeting?"

Successful people love to pay it forward, and successful people in our profession become leaders in their communities with a wealth of knowledge on how to follow in their footsteps. Build your confidence and build the meeting-scheduling muscle. It will pay dividends.

Advisors deal with complex, consequential matters, so the need for ability and expertise is clear. But the confidence part is just as vital. People who lack confidence seem less trustworthy because they don't fundamentally trust *themselves*. They're also not truly others-focused because they're too preoccupied with their own insecurities.

As leaders, our job is to help advisors get further in their lives and careers than if they weren't working with us. In addition to building a company culture with the right core drive and motivations, that means building both confidence and ability among our team so they can better trust themselves and also earn the trust of clients.

Industry leaders often assume that advisors should demonstrate a certain level of proven results before we hire them. They try to find and attract advisors who are already clearly successful. They offer them more pay, more recognition, or a more "fun" work environment—whatever the recruitment pitch is.

While that may make sense on the surface, it also reflects an absence of leadership. If your whole strategy is to hire people who are already amazing and just set them to work, you may have succeeded as a recruiter, but what have you done as a leader? You must help people get further with you than they were able to get without you. This is true of experienced and inexperienced hires.

Besides, there simply aren't enough people out there already trained to do what we do for us to truly grow and scale our firms with experienced advisors alone—let alone those already performing at a high level of both ability and confidence. According to a report by Cerulli Edge, the number of financial advisors only grew by 2,579 in 2022, with a more than 72 percent failure rate among rookies.[7] This is in addition to the fact that over 106,000 advisors plan to retire in the next ten years.

In the last chapter, we talked about building trust with clients by asking questions and meeting them where they are. As a

---

[7] Gregg Greenberg, "Not enough rookie advisors to go around, Cerulli says," *InvestmentNews*, June 26, 2023, https://www.investmentnews.com/industry-news/news/not-enough-rookie-advisors-to-go-around-cerulli-239166.

leader, apply that same logic to new advisors. To start, we have to make it about our team, not about us as leaders.

Don't Be a Hero

To build ability and confidence in our advisors, we have to let them make mistakes—and also let them correct and repair their own missteps. This isn't always easy for leaders. We have a lot of personality-driven leaders in our business, and they love being the hero who swoops in and takes over when things go wrong (then take credit for saving the day).

However, all they've done is further erode their advisors' confidence and ability by making it all about them as the leaders rather than about the advisors themselves. There will always be deadlines and deals to close, but the compound impact of training able and confident advisors outweighs these issues, taking the pressure off individual sales as they develop thriving practices.

When we swoop in to play the hero, we rob advisors of opportunities to grow and build confidence. This stunts their progress and prolongs their learning curve. When we don't lead advisors to a level of both confidence and ability fast enough, they're far more likely to give up. It's been my observation that very few advisors truly "fail" in this business. Among those who leave, most quit before they've genuinely succeeded *or* failed. There's an expiration date to every advisor's career-building phase. Within that finite window of time, we have to be both efficient and effective.

The more effective *others-focused* leader would instead see the problem as an opportunity to coach their advisor. It may be less efficient than just fixing the problem yourself, but it's an invaluable and necessary investment. Most parents understand that they'll never teach their kids new skills if they just do everything for them. Yes, it can be time-consuming and frustrating to teach and coach, but that's the nature of the job. And it's how we build the kind of confidence and ability that grows out of self-trust.

Question the Status Quo

I've already mentioned the status quo practice of hiring only for demonstrated results and why it's both helpful and necessary to think outside of that box. This reflects just one common misguided practice. The truth is that when you look through the lens of "this is what we've always done," you're going have a lot of blind spots.

In particular, I've heard a lot of industry leaders say, "I keep giving advisors this direction, and they're not doing it." My response? Maybe stop trying to do the same thing over and over again, while expecting different results. Let's instead start by examining why the team's not taking your directions.

Being a leader—especially one who trains other leaders—is *not* about making carbon copies of yourself. Unfortunately, not everyone realizes that, which helps explain why so much about our business is stuck in 1950. Strict early morning training sessions. Mandating that advisors show up to a physical office for eight to ten hours a day, five days a week. Adhering to sales training that is all about the numbers game and ego. These are all outdated practices perpetuated by the fear of change and increasingly disconnected from our clients' realities. (Believe it or not, I sadly witnessed a training session where the leader gave the powerful tip to "make sure you compliment the wife" when meeting a client for the first time. I felt embarrassed for him.)

What about our business prevents us from adapting to more flexible, remote, or asynchronous work patterns? If you ask me, it all comes down to a lack of innovative and effective others-focused leadership.

When you hire only according to strict, pattern-matching requirements, then send everyone through the same gatekept, cookie-cutter training protocols, you're dooming your firm and our industry to stagnation. Ironically, it also defies the core tenets of what makes advisors most valuable: our ability to adapt and customize an approach tailored to meet the unique needs of every client.

If you try to make everyone operate exactly as you do, especially if you "lead with a stick," you risk further degrading advisors' confidence in themselves. Basically, you're telling them not to trust their own intuition and to expect punitive measures if they make mistakes. This leads to more insecurity, self-doubt, and the kind of burnout belying our industry's high turnover rates.

Finally, if we keep churning out the same pattern of overbearing leaders and a revolving door of short-term-focused, sales-based advisors, how can we meaningfully meet our clients where they are, which is not in the 1950s?

If we only ever follow the same reasoning from decades ago, never zooming out to reexamine the status quo, we get caught in an endless generational loop that holds back our advisors, harms our public image, and prevents our clients from reaching their full financial potential.

It's time to get nimbler—and humbler. A lot of established professionals scoff when younger generations expect their voices to be heard at the table. I'd argue that as technological and market changes keep accelerating, we need fresh, young perspectives now more than ever. To serve this next generation of clients, we need to first and foremost *understand* them.

If you look at any aspect of human history, it's clear that everything's constantly evolving. As the common phrase goes, "What got us here won't get us there." When your overarching story is that "this is how it's worked for the last fifty years," you're already running on fumes. There's an expiration date for old ways, and I'd say we're long past it.

To build confidence and ability in our advisors, we need to listen to their needs and suggestions. Let's meet advisors where they are, consider their feedback and perspectives, and empower them to really own their careers, their mistakes and wins, and, above all, their own client relationships.

Lessons from the Dream Manager

Most leaders will say that their main priority is "getting results." But while you might get some results from hitting your head against a brick wall, you'll get a lot more if you evolve.

One perspective that changed my view on leadership came from a book by Matthew Kelly called *The Dream Manager.* Kelly's approach aims to improve productivity and job satisfaction in the workplace by focusing not just on results related to quarterly sales metrics or the company's bottom line but also on helping employees identify and achieve their own dreams.

He centers his book around the fictional company, Janitorial Solutions, which struggles to improve morale and combat high employee turnover. The company decides to hire a "dream manager," someone who meets with each worker to discuss their vision of an ideal career and future, then help them plan and execute concrete steps toward fulfilling those dreams.

Kind of sounds like what we do with our clients, doesn't it? We ask them about their ideal financial future, then help them put in place the right strategies for getting there. Applying this same logic to leading advisors helps us understand that worker morale isn't just about titles, paychecks, and ping-pong tables in the breakroom (or these days how many YETIs with logos you own). It's deeply personal to each individual.

In Kelly's narrative, implementing this "dream manager" approach revolutionized the work culture at Janitorial Solutions. By showing specific interest in each employee's dreams and helping them fulfill the same, the company decreased annual worker turnover from 400 percent—costing the company over $2 million per year—to just over 50 percent . . . in only *two years*. While this example is fictional, it's based on a composite of actual companies Kelly has worked with, and this figure reflects the average impact of his approach.

The four-year retention rate in our own industry currently hovers around an abysmal 15 percent. Imagine how much more impact we could have if we increased this number to above 70 percent. That happens to be the published, public goal for our firm, Forest Hills Financial Group. After hovering around 50 percent for a while, we managed to increase that to 54 before this book's publication. The remaining distance to 70 percent will require ongoing discipline, hard work, and a lot of trust.

To achieve this goal, I encourage leaders to implement "dream manager" logic early and often. When potential advisors interview with you, ask them about their professional dreams. Then, discuss potential strategies that you could help implement to get them there—because their success brings your success.

That same logic applies to both clients and advisors alike. It turns out that focusing directly on the success of those you support is, miraculously, also the most effective, efficient way to achieve success for yourself.

The reason Kelly's "dream management" style works so well is that it taps into what each worker finds genuinely motivating, while validating their own unique strengths and goals. This serves to improve advisor engagement in our firms by bolstering their confidence in themselves and helping them gain both confidence and ability.

Diversity and Adaptability

I once attended a leadership conference with some of the most successful leaders in the profession. I remember one speaker telling us, "You could hire anyone to be in this business."

Then he paused and added, "Except I've never hired anyone from the arts."

Three of us in the room that day had professional backgrounds in the arts—including a former musical theater actor, a former ballet dancer, and myself. Together with our partners, we are each responsible for hundreds of advisors and millions of dollars of revenue each year at our firms today.

This gentleman had every right to share his personal experience. He'd earned his reputation as an icon in the profession, having built one of the most successful firms in our system. He also was just stating a fact—and in spite of that particular comment, I appreciated his mentorship. But again, "What got us here will not get us there." If he were in the business today, I have no doubt that he would have had to adapt to the new face of the profession: the diversity, transparency, and energy that a broader community brings.

To take a leap into a profession that deviates from their experience and/or does not reflect their background or community, our future advisors have to trust both their leaders and, most importantly, *themselves*. Without fellow artists in the audience that day, I might have questioned whether or not this career was right for me. We have to be careful of how our words and actions may help or hinder the journeys of others. Some of our greatest talent opportunities can be found among those communities least represented within our industry.

To attract more impact-driven, others-centered people to our business, we have to build public trust—public trust in both the future advisors we attract and the clients they aim to serve. One way to do so is to better reflect the demographics and experiences of the general public—not just the same advisor profiles we've cycled through for decades.

If increasing diversity is one of your firm's goals, how do you attract and build the trust of people who come from less traditional backgrounds? How do you communicate with those individuals? Finally, how do you help them trust themselves enough to confidently and ably guide clients to their best financial outcomes?

Have you thought about that?

One thing's for sure, we can't create a more diverse workforce by doing things the way we've always done them. When considering and interviewing applicants, a lot of leaders ask questions like, "Can this person sell? Can they generate revenue for the firm?" Instead, we should be asking, "What would it take for this person to own their market? What resources do we need in place to support them?"

I get the logic. Pursuing purely transactional goals may help your company in the moment, but it could also be harming your long-term results, making it impossible to meet the kind of retention goals I mentioned above (70 percent) or cultivate long-term relationship continuity with clients. This kind of approach may also prevent a broader mix of people from coming to the table, including those others-focused individuals naturally driven by positive impact.

Why not evaluate the people we interview for their ability to be coached or their desire to build relationships that support their client's long-term financial success? What about their access to broader professional markets based on their educational backgrounds or prior careers? What do we lose when we only look through a transactional lens born from quarterly earnings reports, performance contests, and year-end results?

Next, we have to think about how we manage the advisors we hire. For example, this idea that whoever's not at training at 8:30 a.m. sharp gets locked out of the room. Again, I understand the old-school rationale behind discipline and an early start to the day. But why do we insist on only viewing our industry through that one narrow, outdated lens—ignoring the fact that valuable professionals may be attracted to this career in part because they want flexibility. Many extremely driven, valuable professionals also want to show up for their kids' soccer games and see them off on the bus each morning. Besides, highly capable and professional adults don't need some work "nanny" to motivate them to get up in the morning. We frequently promote the flexibility of the career, but how often do we actually stand behind that?

Years later, when I built my first firm from the ground up, none of our training sessions started before 9:30 a.m. The first person to thank me for that was actually a dad whose wife worked in a less flexible career with a strict early morning schedule. When we think outside the box to support advisors like we support clients, we can all feel the compound impact. The former rigid approach only excludes and eliminates. Meanwhile, flexibility doesn't prevent the early birds from getting a head start. But it does cast a wider net for talent, inviting different experiences and perspectives to the table.

Years ago, when I missed that training session because of my son's daycare drop-off, I initially went along with the logic—both about why the training schedule was so strict and also the notion that I'd "gotten out of" something.

Then, I realized that missing training did me no favors and that there was no particular reason for doing things that way. This realization served as a catalyst to change my perspective. Since then, I've kept up this practice of questioning the underlying wisdom behind gatekeeping patterns that keep our industry in a rut and undermine our public trust. I try to apply this critical lens to everything in the business, and it's helped inform my approach to building confidence and ability in advisors.

Again, it all comes down to trust.

Others-Focused Self-Trust

Many times over the years, I've encountered other people who (like me) exhibit an unusually high degree of self-confidence. It can catch people off guard just how assertively we pursue goals and deliver recommendations—even when they're not what people are expecting or feel ready to hear.

I'll never forget hearing a very successful advisor say, "The presence of integrity is what allows me to be direct." He called it "integrity," but to me it's just others-focused financial guidance. If I know that my genuine goal is to have the greatest positive impact on the person I'm talking to, I'm not going to be afraid to say whatever I think will advance that goal. That reads as confidence.

Ability is easy to grow once you have the confidence—the self-trust—down. At that point, it's just a matter of practice and repetition. Luckily, sincerely focusing on others breeds self-confidence.

Years ago, I had a recruiting coach, who has since sadly passed away. One day, he gave me a bit of coaching I will never forget. He said that before he makes a pitch to a board of directors, he likes to call the coordinator to ask for a quick summary of what exactly the board is looking for. If they say, "revenue, innovation, diversity, and results," he shows up with an agenda slide that reads:

1. Revenue
2. Innovation
3. Diversity
4. Results

This example illustrates how all industry leaders could benefit from cultivating an others-focused core drive and promoting this professional superpower in the advisors we hire, train, and guide. By researching his audience and privileging their goals and values—in this case, those of the board—he was able to enter the meeting exuding far more confidence and clarity than his competitors.

This requires leaders to coach their advisors rather than taking over to fix problems. Confidence derives from the self-trust people naturally gain when they're allowed to lead the conversation rather than just observe it, and that confidence will grow more quickly as they learn from their mistakes.

It also means questioning the status quo that holds advisors and leaders to outdated norms and values and instead learning to become others-focused as a leader. One who takes genuine interest in the dreams of both clients and advisors and guides everyone to their greatest potential.

When people lack trust in themselves, they grow more self-focused. Insecurity can easily become a black hole of seeking outside validation, without ever getting to the root of the issue. Instead, advisors or leaders remain hungry for the prize, the praise, or whatever it is they're measuring in hopes that it will fill that hole.

To achieve optimum success for everyone involved, advisors need to develop an extremely high degree of trust with clients. To do so, they need higher-than-average levels of both ability and confidence, and we can help them get there. We can do it by modeling leadership focused on client impact.

Advisors need to earn their clients' trust before they can educate or empower them to make better financial choices. Similarly, as leaders, we need to earn our advisors' trust in us, and then build that trust in *themselves*, so they can effectively guide themselves—and everyone else involved—to the best possible outcomes.

GUT CHECK

Do you resist the urge to be a hero when your advisors ask for help?

How much do you know about your advisors' dreams for the future?

Are you finding ways to serve new communities?

Have you examined your reasons for doing things the same way you always have? What might be the consequences?

CHAPTER 5

ENGAGEMENT *for* ADVISORS

I joined the Rotary Club early in my career, in part because my mother had been a member growing up, and I remember how her affiliation with that group led to deeply meaningful relationships. Beyond that, I really liked their idea of small acts of service having a large global impact. Through simply gathering donations or planning a fundraising lunch, I could be a part of something that brings clean water access to thousands of people on another continent, while at the same time cleaning up the highway in my own backyard.

For both professional and personal reasons, I was also looking to build trusted relationships based on something authentic and meaningful. As a Canadian-born newcomer and single mom, I needed to connect with other grown-up humans; as a young professional in a heavily referral-based field, I needed to become a known quantity in my community.

To build a truly impact-driven career in financial guidance, conventional marketing is not my preferred path. In our business, I prefer authentic *engagement*—based on trust and a mutual exchange of real value.

Just as you ask for recommendations when finding a new doctor or investing in major car repairs, people turn to those they trust for financial advice. To people whom they have built trust with in completely different ways, usually over many years. Unlike my new colleagues, I couldn't rely on my most trusted network of friends and family. I may have thirty-two first cousins on the other side of our northern border, but we were unable to transact in the securities business internationally (and my local friends were mostly musicians still looking for steady work).

As the daughter of a former Rotary Club president, I knew full well that this was not a professional networking group. You don't come to Rotary functions to promote your business. But you do get to build genuine relationships with people, who naturally end up getting to know each other's backgrounds and careers.

Sure enough, after about a year of active volunteering, I got a call from a Rotary friend who happened to serve on the board of a company looking for some financial advice. This person was also an influential community leader with deep roots, a wide network, and a lot of well-earned trust.

Next thing I knew, I was meeting with the board of a company I never could have gained access to alone. First, I learned all I could about their business and financial needs. Then, I answered questions and recommended potential solutions. Although the value I added that day ended up not being actionable at the time, I made a positive impression on the board members, including a c-level leader who personally reached out to ask me to work with her. Before long, more of this company's board members and executives hired me for personal advising. Within a few years, I was also managing a portfolio of investments for the company itself.

More than fifteen years later, that one introductory meeting with a corporate board has turned into a robust referral stream that's still going and growing. Referrals from one board member alone gained me half a dozen new clients. The spouse of one of the company's c-level executives met me at a social event and asked me to manage their portfolio over a burger—despite just meeting me for the first time. That's a level of trust I never could have achieved through marketing alone.

Trust is not a given. It's something you earn, build, and maintain by consistently doing the right thing. While it's important to have the proper designations and letters after your name and a high degree of competence in your field, it's the trust built from showing up on time, acting professional, adding value, and building genuine connections with people that gets you in the door. Beyond this, there's a whole other level of trust that can only come from the right people demonstrating faith in you.

As Stephen M. R. Covey, the author of *The Speed of Trust*, puts it, trust is "the one thing that changes *everything*." It promotes genuine connections, inspiring creative, mutually beneficial collaborations that ripple worlds further and deeper than any transactional exchange. We build trust through small acts of value, spread far and wide, without any promise of value returned. Showing up to volunteer at local and international communities. Reaching out to your inner circle and professional networks alike. Taking the time to educate groups and individuals, without needing to push a product or make a sale.

The knowledge I passed on to that company's board that day didn't directly earn me a dime, but it indirectly brought me lifelong clients and an active, ongoing referral stream. I did that through educating a group of people as a guest consultant, invited by a trusted insider—not by popping out of nowhere, peddling products and showing off my credentials. It has become one of the many conveyor belts of my practice. Some move faster than others, some take a while to get going, but they all contribute a great deal to my practice and to the impact I'm able to have in my community.

To build the kind of trust required to change our field and maximize our positive compound impact, we need to *engage*. To literally, physically, get out there. Not just to shake hands and pass out business cards but to truly become the center of our communities.

From Transaction to Impact

This was how I built my business. Not through conventional marketing—ads, mail campaigns, and cold-calling—but through in-person community involvement with organizations, causes, and people I care about. Naturally, our profession calls this "warm sourcing" connections, in contrast to the "cold sourcing" of ads and cold calls.

I got into the field before online communities and virtual networking platforms enhanced our ability to connect at a distance. Those digital resources certainly help us engage, and, as technology evolves, how we connect and build relationships will continue to morph. Whether via video or hologram conferencing—or something yet to be invented—I believe it will still be necessary to find shared interests and include face-to-face contact to cement that trust.

Before delving into such engagement approaches, first a word about conventional marketing. Marketing tactics, old or new, all require the same thing: that your audience knows they want or need a product you are selling. That's why you see so many personal injury lawyer billboards—it's one situation where the need for legal counsel becomes clear in an instant. Since most people don't go around looking for this season's hot new financial trends, that marketing approach simply doesn't translate to our work. When people do start Googling for a financial product, that tends to mean they've already decided on their course of action. They're more interested in buying a singular product than in asking for financial guidance. While sales can be (and certainly have been) made this way, they result in one-off deals, and every day you start back at square one with another thousand or so strangers to call.

Sure, there are times when people realize they need, say, an insurance product. They get a new car, or they buy or rent a new home. At those moments, they might look through their pile of junk mail looking for deals. But when it comes to *comprehensive financial planning*—the kind needed to maximize long-term positive financial impact—there is rarely a specific moment in time when anyone says, "Today is the day I must begin planning for retirement!" Same goes for saving for college or purchasing life insurance to protect your family.

If you wait until the moment you need these things, you will fail every time. Imagine waiting until the day you retire to start planning for it, or waiting until your kid gets accepted to college to start an educational fund. Most heartbreaking of all, if you wait until you're terminally ill to apply for life insurance, 100 percent of the time, you will be declined.

To build strategies that set clients up for security and success, we must focus on connections and relationships—not on sales goals and marketing schemes. Plus, in working in an industry that's innately mistrusted, we have extra built-in obstacles to overcome. First, we need to warm-source through established, sincere relationships. Second, we need to educate.

When we see that clients could clearly benefit from a solution, but they nevertheless think it's not for them, it's our responsibility to inform and explain. When we educate (on the foundation of trusted relationships) the barriers caused by that deep-seated public distrust begin to break down. Because people are so averse to being sold, we must initially meet them where they are in their financial journey and work diligently to move them along the continuum until they are comfortable taking action on our advice. While this may take more time at the beginning of the relationship, the benefit will come later, as your future interactions and referrals begin to move at the "speed of trust." In other words, if you do the hard things first, the rest of your life will be easier.

The vast majority of advisors understand and appreciate this idea of adding value through customized, comprehensive planning. Still, each time the phone rings and a potential client says, "I want to open an IRA," they lose sight of the bigger picture. In their rush to transact, they do the easy thing first, which I promise will make the rest of your work very hard. Instead, try saying, "Let's carve out some time to sit down, look at your overall situation, and figure out the best approach for your goals."

I'm not saying, "Never be transactional." Making sales forms part of that guidance and support. What I am saying is, "Be comprehensive." Taking a comprehensive approach does not exclude helping people solve a particular need at a particular time. But a transactional strategy that lacks follow-through impedes both your clients' success and the impact of your work. If you never expose your clients to the full extent of what's possible, they will not get the best advice, and you may prevent them from seeking or receiving the additional help they need. This is the harmful side of compound impact—the ripple effects that come from incomplete plans and half-baked strategies.

You will more readily build relationships and earn your reputation as a trusted advisor if you bother to take the more comprehensive, impact-driven approach. Learn all you can about their situation, help them envision their optimal financial success, and educate them about every opportunity to make that vision a reality.

Surprise! Warm Sourcing Is Not About You

We often train advisors to build as many relationships as possible with accountants and attorneys in their communities. That's because accountants and attorneys both build long-term relationships with their clients, and, for the most part, they build their practices through referrals. Like us, they may not be well-trusted among the general public, but the clients they've built relationships with over time tend to count them among their most trusted advisors. Like us, it's more effective for accountants and attorneys to build their businesses through referrals than it is to gain the public's trust directly through marketing campaigns.

That doesn't mean you should reach out to lawyers and CPAs and immediately push your firm or brag about your achievements. Just like when you sit down with clients, warm sourcing is not about you—it's about the other people.

When talking to attorneys, accountants, or any influential contacts, take a deep dive into what they do, how they run their business, and their short- and long-term goals and vision. Then, ask yourself this: How can *you*, as an advisor, create value for *them*? Can you introduce them to someone in a critical community, field, or network? Can you send some business their way? Can you educate them on something of interest to them or their firm? The initial engagement is always about learning and understanding—then bringing value. Quite frequently, that value will have nothing to do with what *you* get paid for.

Related to my earlier comment about billionaires, successful businesspeople tend to be better at delegating. In fact, they're always actively looking for people to delegate to and opportunities to off-load tasks. They understand that the more effectively they delegate, the more time and energy they free up to focus on the unique abilities "at the top of their license," which helps them scale their businesses. There's an entire cottage industry of business coaching dedicated to the art of delegation. As advisors, we develop relationships to earn the privilege of having clients delegate their essential financial planning to us.

That's the essence of warm sourcing. It's all about prioritizing others and establishing trust. Warm sourcing builds on preexisting relationships to earn the privilege of having a conversation with someone about what you do. Just as you need to be patient and curious with clients (rather than skipping straight to sales), take your time when building a network—and make it about *them*.

Unexpected Ripples

You've likely heard the term "orphans" to refer to clients whose advisors have retired or left the field. One of my best examples of the ripple effects of genuine client engagement involved a couple of "orphans"—partners who co-owned an accounting firm. Let's call them Ayana and Eli.

These two wanted advice about life insurance policies they'd bought as a buy-sell agreement, meaning that if something happened to one business partner, the other would receive insurance proceeds sufficient to buy the other partner's half of the business from their estate.

A few years into their partnership, Ayana and Eli decided to buy the building they'd been renting for their firm. Because their life insurance policies had cash value, they were able to take loans against the policies to buy the building. Now, they were paying back those loans—and having doubts.

During our first conversation, they explained that they wanted to cancel the policies to avoid having to pay back the loan. Now, to be clear, I didn't stand to make any money whether these people kept their policies or canceled them. From a purely transactional approach, I could have taken their phone call and simply said, "You probably won't need life insurance. Go ahead and cancel the policies. Here's a form."

But I couldn't say that—not in good faith. Canceling a life insurance policy is like taking a bucket of cash with your loved ones' names on it and tossing it in the dumpster because you want the bucket for something else. So I said, "Why don't I come up and sit down with you before you take any action either way to make sure you understand your options fully?"

These days, it might be just as effective to schedule a Zoom call, but that was before widespread video meetings, so I drove about an hour and a half to sit down with them, fully engage, and learn about their accounting firm. I explained to them the value of keeping the policies, even though there would be no compensation for me.[8] (In fact, I lost money paying for gas.)

Being the intelligent professionals they were, at the end of the meeting, they said, "All of that makes sense. I think we won't cancel them . . . but why are you doing this? You don't get paid on any of this."

I answered honestly: "You're both CPAs with successful practices," I said. "I'm starting to build my business. If I can add value for you now, maybe at some point in the future there will be a way that I can help one of your clients."

The impact of this warm-sourcing engagement was two-fold: first, the compound impact on Ayana and Eli (and their families) and second, the compound impact on my practice.

Let's start with Ayana and Eli. A few years after our conversation, and after they'd fully paid back their insurance-based loans, I got a call from Ayana saying she had been diagnosed with a fatal nervous system disease. Over the following eighteen months, I helped Ayana get her affairs in order for her

---

[8] The primary feature of whole life insurance is the death benefit. Policy loans and withdrawals affect the guarantees by reducing the policy's death benefit and cash values. Some whole life policies do not have cash values in the first two years of the policy and don't pay a dividend until the policy's third year.

family and her business. Eli again borrowed against the cash value of his side of their life insurance policies in order to buy out Ayana's share of the business. In effect, Eli gave his partner the cash value from his life insurance, and in exchange, Ayana gave Eli the practice. This allowed Ayana to step away from the business instantly and spend the final eighteen months of her life doing what mattered most: spending time with the people she loved.

When Ayana passed away, her business had been settled, and her husband and kids received the proceeds of her insurance policy. You can already see how far this policy went toward solving problems, and that's not even the end of the story.

Eli again repaid the loan to keep his life insurance policy. After a while, he decided to buy a second home in South Carolina. So he again borrowed against the policy to buy the second home with a cash payment—without having to go to the bank. As he got closer to retirement, he and his wife downsized from their primary home, which was not quite ready to sell. So, one final time, they used the cash value of their repaid policy to buy a smaller townhome before his primary residence was sold.

From that first conversation fifteen years ago, this one insurance product prevented Eli from losing a business, gave Ayana the precious gift of spending her final days with family without worrying about finances, and facilitated three real estate loans. Not only that, but the policy can still someday fulfill its intended purpose when Eli's family needs it. He could still use the cash value again—for example, if the market is in terrible shape and he wants to avoid a downturn. Of course, he also still has the option of canceling it, but after all that, who would do such a thing?

If I had answered the phone all those years ago and just said, "I'll send you the form you need to cancel your policy," think of what those ripple effects would have been. How might that have impacted Ayana's life and family? What about Eli's business and family? For an apparent no-value visit, that one conversation made an invaluable, ongoing impact.

The other side of this story was its impact on me as an advisor. I could have saved time and gas that day. I could have said to myself, *These are not even my clients. Who cares about orphans? I need to just get off the phone as fast as I can so that I can find someone who will buy today.* If that had been my perspective, there would have been a lot of fairly invisible—yet utterly catastrophic—ripple effects.

Instead, the positive effects extended to me and my practice. After our initial chat, both Ayana and Eli both occasionally turned to me for minor, immediate financial advice. After Ayana passed, I helped manage the money her family had inherited. Prior to her passing, Ayana had written letters to each of her family members, introducing me to them and expressing her wishes that they work with me when she was gone. Those letters reminded me of the great honor bestowed on us as advisors to carry out the legacies of our clients.

In Eli's case, I ended up helping him and his wife build their investment portfolios. Perhaps the biggest value for our firm came through the quality of these clients' referrals. Ayana and Eli both connected me to multiple new clients who needed help with retirement accounts, investment accounts, insurance policies, and even a large family trust.

It would have been so easy to *not* do the right thing, especially when it came to a couple of "orphans" whose finances were not my responsibility and whose decision either way wouldn't directly affect me.

I didn't see it that way. I saw it as an opportunity to genuinely engage and add value. Even when you can't see what you're going to get out of the interaction, the value of building trust is much, much greater than the value of getting paid to process a transaction.

Becoming the Center of Your Community

There are many ways to increase your direct, meaningful engagement within a community: volunteering, hosting educational speaking events, joining professional networking groups, and even reaching out to your inner circle. Each approach involves a give and a take.

Volunteering & Donating

Let's start with volunteering. When you give your time, effort, and talents in this way, you gain both awareness and alignment. You learn more about a cause you care about and a need within the community. You also gain awareness of the people impacted by that need, as well as the associated opportunities and roadblocks. Finally, you align with real people who care about the same things you do, just like I did with the Rotary Club.

This deeper alignment puts you in a great position to eventually explain what you do to people you resonate with. When you spend time asking questions and taking interest in others, they will do the same in return. Then you get the chance to demonstrate the scope of the work that you do, the people whom you help, and the value that you provide.

Having given them your full attention and respect, you earn theirs in return. Once you establish trust and create value for other professionals, you're more uniquely qualified to help them and their contacts than other advisors with less insight into that community.

When you first start out, you're more likely to donate in terms of time and effort. But once you've established yourself and gained enough personal resources, you'll be able to contribute even further to these causes through charitable giving, so make sure you are getting involved in causes genuinely important to you. By donating some of your own financial resources, you can similarly gain awareness and alignment with those who share your interests and values, allowing you to provide more mutual value.

Education

Educational opportunities typically involve speaking engagements, whether at a professional conference, local book club, informal business "lunch and learn," panel discussion, or webinar. The purpose is to impart knowledge and open the audience members' minds to new concepts—*not* to give advice, which at this stage would be far too premature.

One of the biggest problems with the influencers, celebrity advisors, and talking heads is that they're trying to give advice when they should be imparting knowledge. People may call or write in asking questions about specific tips and strategies, but they share little to no context when it comes to their comprehensive financial goals and situation. Not only can this be incredibly harmful to the person asking the question (if the answer is not best-suited for their bigger picture goals) but now other listeners who hear that specific, out-of-context advice may go on to apply it to their own lives—without ever talking things over with a qualified, trustworthy advisor. The potentially negative ripple effects of these practices boggle the mind.

I don't think it's an overstatement to say that I consider it malpractice to give advice without first fully and privately gathering facts and data. Imagine a doctor just walking into the waiting room and saying, "Everyone gets a prescription for this medication. It's good for you! Drugs for everyone!" No intake. No questions. No bloodwork.

When you have the opportunity to speak to a group, remember that you're there to provide context and ideas, not to make recommendations. A speaking engagement or panel discussion is not the time to push specific products or solutions, but rather to speak at a higher level about what we do and why.

Occasionally, it might make sense to address specific topics or solutions, but beyond describing the general context for these things, always emphasize that they are matters best explored *with a personal advisor*. You could speak about financial balance, protection (as a general concept), compound interest, the tax statuses of various investment accounts, the impact of waiting to save, or the misnomer that people think they can't afford to hire a financial advisor until they've amassed considerable wealth. Publicly debunking common harmful misconceptions adds clear value to consumers, clients, and to our field in general, but you can only do that if you see these opportunities as just the first step. You will still need to further invest in these relationships and build on the initial opportunities to connect and educate.

Business Networking

Formal educational opportunities are different from business networking. Business networking simply involves reaching out to other professionals and making genuine connections.

We all do this all the time—not just when we go to group networking events but also when we take the time to really connect with people we may be able to refer clients to, and vice versa. Beyond CPAs and attorneys, we often look to mortgage brokers, realtors, community leaders, and other centers of influence in their respective fields.

When networking with other professionals, keep your focus on building relationships and gaining trust. This means hanging those ears on the end of your bell by thinking first and foremost—even solely—about *them* and how you can add value through information, resources, referrals, or introductions. Once you've done that, it's fair and reasonable to schedule another meeting to share the scope of the work you do and the value it adds to people's lives.

Networking is a process. Rarely will attending a singular event generate business. My recommendation is that you focus on finding engaging groups, associations, or communities that meet regularly. Find a way to get involved—in a committee, on the board, or as a volunteer. The more involved you become, the stronger the relationships you are building will be.

Inner Circle

Finally, let's talk about your personal life and inner circle. Many new and prospective advisors say they are interested in the career but not interested in working with family and friends.

They find it awkward to talk to people close to them about money, not wanting to mix business with their personal lives.

To that, I say, if the foundation of what we do is build trust to help people maximize their financial success, wouldn't you want to help the people you care about most?

Think for a moment about public perception. Would you want to work with someone who refuses to offer their expertise to family and friends? There's something potentially sketchy about that, if you ask me. It suggests a possible lack of integrity or that there is something wrong with the products and services they provide. At a minimum, it says that the advisor does not truly believe in the work that they do.

Let's say you're a medical researcher working on a cure for a specific kind of cancer, and you develop a treatment that has great success in early trials. Then someone in your family gets diagnosed with that specific cancer. Would you keep it a secret that there's a potential solution to prolong their life or cure their disease?

You might. But only if you believed the risk of harming them outweighed the promise of helping them. If so, that should provide some feedback on how you really feel about this thing you're developing—or in our case, selling. What would it mean if you're okay with exposing strangers to this risk but not family or friends?

As an advisor, I personally do work with close friends and family, and I approach them like any other clients. I learn everything I can about their situation and goals; I educate them on the best, most comprehensive strategy for getting there; then I let them decide.

That said, I always emphasize that advisors should avoid confusing social time with business time. What we do is serious business, and it requires a professional setting. As with the COIs, find a way to add value and find an appropriate time to ask them if they would be willing to sit down and learn about the work that you do.

Examining your stance on working with friends and family offers a great way to "gut check" your own integrity—similar to the question about what you do for a living and what you *say* you do. On the flip side, if you don't want your clients to see or know anything about your personal life, what does that indicate about your trustworthiness? The greater the dissonance between those two spheres of life, the greater the chances that you're not fully aligned to a client-centered, impact-driven approach.

Whether or not you work with family and friends, you want your clients to feel authentically connected to you, to trust you with their personal information and to guide them through major decisions. They don't have to become your closest friends, but you should literally—authentically—care about these people and their outcomes (and when you do, you'll find that they tend to care about you in return).

Authentic Connections

When either officially networking or reaching out professionally to your inner circle, warm sourcing often means giving up some of the compartmentalization between work and life. You make your public life more private, and vice versa. While work should never take over your life, you don't need to protect your friends and family from what you do (provided it's actually valuable). There can—and I think there should—be some overlap. At the very least, your work life and home life should mutually align.

Think of the old model of the breadwinner father coming home, sitting down to dinner, and never talking to his family about what he does at work (or about finances, for that matter) at all. These days, we work and live differently. People increasingly want careers that compliment or even integrate more into the fabric of their lives.

To build trust, you need to be both trustworthy and easy to get along with. A big part of building professional (and personal) trust comes down to authentically representing yourself and your work and enjoying your interactions. Imagine if, five years from now, you were so thrilled with your career that you genuinely looked forward to seeing every single one of your clients on the calendar. Who would those people be? What would they do for a living? What would they do for fun? What characteristics and traits (having nothing to do with their money) would make you feel that you could relate to them and become a part of their community?

There are so many ways to become the center of your community. The options extend well beyond joining the Rotary Club, advising your family, and speaking at events. You should do what helps you form connections and adds value to an ever-widening network of people whom you genuinely like and care about.

By all means, innovate new ways and try new vectors. Each of these engagement methods involves giving something (time, privacy, etc.) and gaining something (awareness, alignment, etc.). It's not so much about the specific method of direct engagement as about the intentions and principles of *adding value*—to build a solid network of relationships based on authenticity and trust.

GUT CHECK

What opportunities do you have to spread the impact of your work—to extend that ripple throughout your community?

What community organizations do you feel most aligned with and eager to support?

Are you willing to reach out to close friends and family to help them with their finances?

What opportunities do you have to educate local groups about what we do?

CHAPTER 6

ENGAGEMENT *for* LEADERS

I once hired an advisor named Jason, who'd switched careers after more than a decade in pharmaceutical sales. In many ways, it was a cushy job, one he'd scored right after getting his MBA from a prestigious school. He earned six figures and drove a company car—constantly crisscrossing the state to sit in parking lots waiting to make his ten-minute sales pitches to busy physicians.

Jason may have been able to provide well for his family, but after ten-plus years, he was exhausted, overworked, demoralized, and tired of spending so much time away from home. His work depended on sales timelines for different pharmaceutical drugs. When each timeline ran out, he'd have to get on the phone to figure out if he still had a job. Motivation tactics relied heavily on the stick—and on fierce competition—with few carrots in sight and no real growth trajectory. The compensation difference between the highest and lowest performers came to maybe $5,000 a year.

Like many professionals who feel they've hit some kind of a ceiling, Jason had a real desire to use his professional sales training to help him transition into a more personally fulfilling career that would allow him to spend more time at home and have a true impact on his community. As he put it, he wanted to feel like he was on the other side of the desk—in a role that more resembles what doctors do rather than sales reps.

As he saw it, our field offered more of the long-term relationship building and potential for impact that Jason wanted. He spent time researching and interviewing and even sat for his licenses in preparation for this move, but at first, it went nowhere. He felt like all companies were offering was a phone book and a directive: "Get out there and make some calls. You know doctors, so you'll be successful."

That didn't sound like much of a change in terms of personal fulfillment or community impact. While Jason had close relationships with some of the doctors he called on, he hesitated to make a major career change just to end up fighting the same battles. He didn't just want to grow professionally and financially but also wanted the real connections and sense of purpose that comes from having a positive impact on others.

When Jason switched to financial advising, he was making the choice to quit his six-figure job in the only field he knew (aside from the ice cream truck he drove in college). When he made that leap, a corporate representative flew in the very next day, took the keys to his company car and his corporate credit card, and drove away. He looked at his wife, sank into the sofa, and said, "Did I just bankrupt us?"

All of this to say that the move into this career was not easy. But he took a chance and made the shift because he desperately wanted to apply his skills toward engaging with people and adding value to their lives, all within a field where he, himself, could feel wholeheartedly engaged and valued.

I hired and trained Jason, who went on to become a very successful advisor, leader, and influential member of his community. Recently, I also attended a milestone birthday party, where I got to chatting with some of his closest friends.

When I explained who I was, they stopped short, glanced at each other, and grinned. One of them said, "Wait, you're Amy? You changed his life."

That remains one the most meaningful compliments I've ever received.

Jason knew he wasn't changing lives by talking to doctors about drugs. Now, he gets a chance to change some of those doctors' lives (among others). Luckily for Jason and his clients, an impact-driven professional who thrives on building relationships and guiding others toward success is exactly what our profession needs.

When I met Jason, I assured him he'd get all the training to gain requisite technical skills and succeed in this business. We would teach him how to find and develop a market that he would be proud to work with for years to come. That allowed him to take the leap, and he never looked back. While the start of any financial advisor's career has its ups and downs, he advanced quickly, accelerated his trajectory, and found a career for life. Most of all, he's forged authentic relationships with hundreds of clients whose lives would not be the same if he hadn't become their advisor.

If I'd taken the approach of only hiring demonstrably successful financial advisors, I might have passed up his application as lacking in directly relevant experience. If I'd sounded more like the firms that Jason passed up (to accept our offer), we might have similarly turned him off of our company. If I'd hired him and pushed traditionally aggressive sales goals and cold-calling, I could have easily disillusioned him with the field once he saw how the work culture mirrored the one he'd just escaped. In any of these cases, he never would have impacted the lives and families of the hundreds of clients he now serves.

As leaders, it's not as simple as attracting "top talent" and saying, "Get out there and make some calls!" To build a team of highly engaged advisors, we have to help them evolve and navigate mental shifts, as advisors and as leaders themselves. Finally, we have to hold true to the promise that this profession promotes freedom, growth opportunities, and the chance to truly make a difference.

Sourcing

When looking for prospective advisors, as with anything else, if we keep doing what we've always done, we will get what we've always gotten: appallingly low retention rates and continued pressure to recruit for volume rather than quality.

To start, examine the descriptions in your job posts. Do they capture the impact-focused nature of our work? Are you clearly expressing your ability to train and develop market-building skills to attract people from various backgrounds? Do your postings appeal to a diverse group of candidates reflecting your local communities?

If not, there's a great opportunity to better engage and recruit—and don't worry, you're not the only one. Most job postings for financial advisors mainly push product sales, while emphasizing the money candidates can make if they just throw enough spaghetti at the wall. I know what I see, and I know what I hear, and the picture too often painted reflects neither the business I believe I'm in, nor any business I want to be a part of.

Engagement extends to all parts of our work. As leaders, we want to engage our internal communities of advisors by providing true value to them. For us, being client-centric means being advisor-centric. In addition to the impact we bring to their lives, proof of our success will come through introductions to other candidates from within our ranks. If we are doing a great job of supporting our advisors, they will recommend others to us.

We also need to engage communities outside our firms, both to grow our outreach and client base and to attract new advisors. To do this, we can use the very same practices discussed in the last chapter to increase advisor engagement in the community—but with a lens toward finding and gaining referrals for candidates driven by impact.

Culture over "Killers"

When interviewing potential advisors, I've noticed an increase in questions about work culture. In addition to vision and strategic planning, candidates want to know about core values. They want a good fit—a sense of belonging—because they want to feel genuinely engaged at work.

I like it when I see that because those are typically also people who engage well with others. The ones who build relationships, contribute to a positive culture, and understand what it means to become the center of their community.

Unfortunately, the traditional recruiting approach leans toward candidates with a demonstrated "killer instinct." Low call reluctance. High tolerance for rejection. Keep people talking. Convince consumers of "what's in it for them." Push the sales. With this shark mentality, you don't need to lead with integrity, or even with warmth. I interviewed someone the other day who told me they made ten thousand phone calls and only got three clients! Not only is this highly inefficient, but it borders on masochism.

It's still what many firms look for, and it's still what a lot of candidates lead with: "I'm fiercely competitive, I can sell anything, and I have good math skills."

What I always want to know next is: How good are you at listening, building authentic relationships, and personalizing advice to the best interests of clients? Can you guide people with both transparency and integrity? Are you genuinely confident or do you just play a confident person on TV?

Human Data—and Connections

Looking toward the future, we need to build firms that can thrive in the world of AI. This means adding value to clients that extends far beyond mere product sales. According to an alarming 2024 "full-service investor satisfaction survey" by J.D. Power, a full 41 percent of client experiences in the US fall into the "transactional" category.[9] This is not good, when you consider that this area of our business faces the highest risk of being replaced by new technology. In terms of simply delivering products without any corresponding advice, we cannot compete with AI.

[9] "Satisfaction Rises among Clients Using Financial Advisors," *The Wealth Advisor*, March 21, 2024, https://www.thewealthadvisor.com/article/satisfaction-rises-among-clients-using-financial-advisors.

To thrive in our profession, we must know our value and how to communicate it. We have to recruit and train *financial advisors*, not transactional salespeople. We can't out-expert Google when it comes to pure information retention. Search engines already store the sum of the world's information. We can, however, help clients synthesize that information, put it in order, and advise on next steps in our pursuit of the best possible outcomes for each individual client. That is why clients gravitate to us, compared to one-size-fits-all robo-advisors.

Let's also look beyond mere product savvy and the ability to do swift mental calculations. There's no shortage of tools to help us research, analyze, and build custom portfolios. Yes, we need people who can track results and interpret data—and we can also use AI to help us access all that information efficiently—but that won't get us too far. Not without the ability to also build relationships and give advice relevant to the *human* aspects of our clients' lives. Beyond their family's basic security, this includes their goals, dreams, loved ones, and legacies.

We need advisors with the ability to synthesize all that information and come up with customized, comprehensive guidance that supports the best possible outcomes for clients. This requires a rare ability to seek out others in need of help, genuinely engage with them, earn the trust required for them to open up, and finally motivate them to take specific action to improve their financial futures.

Consumers and clients increasingly want to understand how things work—and *why*. People don't just come in, hear advice, then unquestioningly sign papers. They want to know why this approach is better than what they found on Google or heard from their neighbor or while listening to a celebrity advisor. They obviously don't want to hear, "Because if you take this strategic advice, it'll help my sales goals."

Hiring for Engagement

Considering public perception, if most people believe that what's needed in this business is a shark mentality, we may predominantly be attracting and hiring the wrong people.

I prefer those candidates who question the way things are done. I love when I can see the wheels start to turn as I describe our emphasis on *engagement* over traditional marketing tactics. We look for advisors eager to learn all they can about the community of clients we guide and support. The ones who aren't afraid to use their voice or receive feedback, training, and guidance themselves.

To attract *this* kind of talent, we need to also lead with transparency and integrity. We can't just say, "This is how you get paid because this is how you get paid." People want to know how things work and to what end. Asking *why* used to be considered insolent. Now it's an asset—a sign of engagement, intelligence, and buy-in.

We're not just slinging stocks in an abstract world of profits, losses, and sales goals. We're dealing with people's lives. We're talking to them about some of the most significant and personal decisions they'll ever make. When it comes to advisors, people need—and increasingly, demand—authentic relationships and personalized, transparent advice. They want actual human engagement with someone who truly cares.

That may sound sappy to some, but brush it aside at your own risk. Given the low public perception of our field—and with so many other competing sources of information—integrity and a genuine concern for others are quickly emerging as top assets within our field.

Next, we have to help our hires become the advisors their clients need and deserve. It's not just about telling them what to do (*because we said so*). It's not about making a million phone calls, playing the numbers game, and schmoozing without really listening. Over the years, I've made the mistake of hiring people who operate that way, and I have seen how the inability to be open and vulnerable, show their human side, and build genuine relationships virtually guarantees failure. It doesn't matter whether they have a background as a professional athlete, an MBA, or an incredible resume. If they cannot genuinely connect with people, this is not the business for them.

According to a 2022 LIMRA report,[10] the vast majority of advisors surveyed felt that our field exceeded expectations in terms of both having the opportunity to make a difference and having good work-life balance. Meanwhile, almost half said that their income expectations were not met.

I find it interesting that when LIMRA and Finseca asked leaders which factors contribute to termination and retention, at least six of the nine most common answers seem to fully blame the candidates.

---

[10] "Improving Financial Professional Retention Requires a Combinations of Rewards and Reality," LIMRA, July 17, 2022, https://www.limra.com/en/newsroom/industry-trends/2022/improving-financial-professional-retention-requires-a-combination-of-rewards-and-reality/.

As I see it, we recruited them and selected them. Therefore, especially if they're new to this business, it is our job to train them. Imagine a professor failing all the students in their general surgery rotation because they didn't already know how to gown up. Prospecting and building a market is foundational—it's the "gowning up" of our business—so we better be able to show new advisors how it's done. When we deny or downplay the impact of management and agency culture or the selection process itself, we're avoiding accountability and ensuring nothing changes.

Training with a Client-Centered Approach

To get highly engaged advisors, start by recruiting for integrity, impact, and relationship building. Then, train your people to give impact-driven, comprehensive, customized advice rather than simply driving sales. We do this by modeling and

[11] Kathleen Krozel, "A Path to Better Agent Retention."

encouraging an others-first engagement style to financial guidance, one that leads to a much larger professional network for our advisors and our firms—and a greater ripple effect for everyone involved.

We can't just train advisors to be sources of information because that's not what clients need anymore. They all have access to Google, where they can type, "How much do I need to retire?" or "How much life insurance do I need?" and get 1.5 million results in 0.3 seconds. Clients hire us because of how we can sift through that information and cater the best integrated plans and solutions to their unique goals and circumstances. Not just standardized search engine results but personalized, client-centered, and impact-driven financial guidance from a *human* expert.

Our entire industry is evolving and shifting. As leaders, we need to help advisors similarly evolve and navigate these shifts. One shift certainly involves technology. As algorithmic digital tools become more prevalent and advanced, they may represent competition for human advisors—but only to a point.

Think of it this way. When people start their first job and sign up for a 401(k), they have no idea how it's invested or what any of it really means. They're so far from retirement that the whole thing is pretty abstract, so whatever the default investment is, they're often fine with that.

But there comes a point where the stakes rise. There will always be a threshold after which people trade standardized, robotic advice for more personalized, comprehensive guidance. That might be $10,000, $100,000, or $1 million—it all depends on the client.

After that point, clients come to humans for financial advice because they're making decisions with sky-high *human* stakes. They don't want to make moves impacting their children's education, their retirement income, or their loved ones' security by plugging data into a form that spits out algorithmic answers. To ensure our advisors are there at the right time, we must train them to forge relationships sooner and communicate to their clients the massive lifelong impact of earlier planning.

Our job is to take advisors and help them skillfully approach and engage clients. When we focus our training on impact, we train for integrity, transparency, and long-term relationship building. In doing so, we help them grow as professionals and as people—particularly if we also take the "dream manager" approach of actually listening to our advisors and integrating their own personal goals and dreams into the equation.

To get more engaged advisors, we need more engaged leaders, especially while training. Make sure you help new advisors understand the particular value of particular products. Paint a picture of the ripple effects—both good and bad—using real-life examples to show client impact.

Share case studies of how advisors using these products first found and got to know their clients. Were they parroting scripted language to set up appointments or communicating real value for their potential clients? Did those clients come in knowing they needed this solution, or did they need skilled guidance to arrive at the solution?

Help advisors understand the art of data gathering: how to avoid assumptions, identify blind spots, and ask great questions. Make sure those questions help your advisors uncover their clients' value system and share examples with them.

When training advisors to make recommendations and improve sales skills, focus less on how advisors can close deals and more on how well they can express how a particular approach or product would benefit clients and if they can motivate others to take action toward their own financial goals. Train them to articulate exactly why a certain recommendation represents the best course of action for the client—not to offer up financial advice that looks like a diner menu. Finally, show your advisors how to consistently reassess a client's circumstances so they can iterate and optimize their approach.

If we approach our training with this level of leader engagement, we automatically improve results, which naturally leads to better retention. When advisors can look back and recognize that their firm's guidance and support helped them progress beyond what they could have done alone, the leaders of that firm gain deep loyalty. Better advisor retention reduces advisor churn and improves efficiency and client impact, but that only happens when we take responsibility to recruit well and train our people to be advisors rather than salespeople. Better retention comes from more authentic human relationships, both among your team and with your clients and community.

In chapter four, I talked about confidence and ability as the core ingredients for self-trust and professional success. When you can authentically engage with your advisors and leaders to help them grow in these areas, they naturally want to stick around.

Navigating Shifts

As impact-driven, client-centered leaders, we have to apply that engagement mentality to our advisors as well as our clients.

We can't go out into the world expecting to have a huge impact, while taking shortcuts to get there. We can't just look for people who already have all the required skills and don't need to learn anything from us, then sit back and take credit for their work. Instead, focus on providing value to your advisors by helping them accomplish more with us that they could on their own.

On the flip side, we can't keep recycling licensed candidates with no track record of success as though we can "save" them. We need to source and engage with future advisors at the level we're asking advisors to engage in their communities.

Above all, we need to live up to our titles as leaders. Are we keeping up with and adapting to market and societal changes? How are we navigating our own mental shifts between "what we've always done" to "what actions will support the best possible positive impact?"

Engaged leadership develops engaged advisors. This also means bringing in candidates who want development, personal growth, and meaningful work. The ones who will become true students of the business, focused on how their work can have the greatest impact. While this may require some patience (impact-driven advisors will not take shortcuts), their engagement will yield tremendous growth overall.

Our top advisors have established successful careers and emerged as inspiring, effective leaders. If we want to scale our companies enough to better serve our communities, we must bridge the gap between brand new advisors and these superstars. That means hiring and training advisors for impact, emphasizing their responsibility to the clients they serve, and developing them to be leaders, not followers.

As advisors, we know our role is to listen to people, meet them where they are, then lead them to a success they couldn't have reached on their own. As leaders, we have to have the same type of impact on our advisors. We have to guide and support them the same way we train them to engage with clients.

When I interviewed Jason more than a decade ago, he felt disillusioned by the stagnant state of his own success. Luckily for all of us, an impact-driven professional who thrives on building relationships and guiding others toward success was exactly what my firm was looking for. And it's exactly what our entire industry urgently needs to evolve and navigate shifts of our own to stay relevant. It's up to us as leaders to recruit and train with that in mind.

For more than a decade, Jason's work has exemplified the commitment and loyalty that naturally follow when you can teach someone how to succeed in the business through client-centered financial guidance. That's not just a win for me and our firm, it's a win for Jason, his family, his hundreds of clients, and all the people impacted by these individuals' success.

GUT CHECK

Are you recruiting for engagement or for sales? How?

How are you engaging those you recruit?

Are you coaching your advisors and leaders to greater heights?

Are your advisors introducing new candidates to the firm?

CHAPTER 7

CHANGE *for* ADVISORS

Wealth building. Retirement security. Income protection and legacy. Emergency funds and rainy day savings. It's hard to argue that these are *bad* things to have. Still, as advisors, we know how often consumers and clients forgo invaluable future benefits for the immediate rewards of shorter-term spending.

"Do I *really* need it?" clients often ask (especially when it comes to insurance products). In my professional and personal opinion, they do. Not in the *exact moment* when they're sitting there talking to me, of course. Much of the success of a financial plan depends on taking action *now* to protect or enrich ourselves and our families in the future, well before unexpected financial setbacks or concerns arise.

Here's the thing, though. According to psychologists, our brains don't actually identify with our future selves, at least not directly. Instead, the concept registers in a detached, hypothetical way—almost as though we're talking about strangers rather than ourselves.

Back in 2011, Harvard professor Jason Mitchell led a study monitoring participants' brains using fMRI scans as they thought about different scenarios, including: 1. Enjoying an event in the present moment, 2. Their future selves enjoying an event, and 3. Other people enjoying the same event. They found that when people thought about themselves in the future, it activated the same parts of the brain that lit up when thinking about *other people*.

Mitchell's studies have been replicated and continued by psychologists and marketing scholars, including UCLA professor Hal Hershfield, who in 2023 published a book called *Your Future Self: How to Make Tomorrow Better Today.* In addition to exercise and diet, Hershfield focuses his research on money management.

This lack in what scholars call "introspective self-reference" about the future helps explain why so many of our clients resist, drain, or cancel life insurance policies, why they slack on retirement planning, and why they delay setting up systematic savings plans. Our clients may logically accept that they will exist and have needs in the future, but the whole idea remains abstract—as though they're talking about someone else's problems, not their own.

It's our job as advisors to get clients to *want* to plan for the future—to take action now to create positive impact years down the line. If you think about the solutions we offer, they're all designed to help clients' futures. To their brains, that can be a tough sell. Not only do clients find it difficult cognitively to identify with future rewards, but we're also not talking about getting their future selves a chic new wardrobe or sleek convertible car; we're talking about insurance policies and other mundane financial security matters. We know (all too well) how much regret and hardship can result when clients resist our advice. Still, when the security of their future selves doesn't feel enticing, it's hard for them to find a compelling reason to act in the present.

Besides, as mentioned before, there's no standard life event or outside force prompting anyone to, say, purchase disability insurance or optimize their savings strategy. There's no external point of reckoning that forces responsibility upon people—just the abstract specter of potential setbacks, disasters, or missed opportunities somewhere down the road. Even when they witness first-hand how insufficient planning can harm a family, such as in the wake of a relative's disability or death, people rarely apply that same logic to themselves. Otherwise, we'd see a rush on our offices to eliminate similar financial risks.

The abstraction of futurity is one of the biggest reasons why it's so hard to change consumer complacency around financial planning. It's also why it's so important for us, as advisors, to make changes ourselves.

If we, as advisors, cannot motivate ourselves to plan for our own professional and financial futures, how can we possibly expect our clients to take action? We need to get away from the default mode of "do as I say, not as I do." This means being your own best client. It's not enough to say, "I have an investment account, and I own insurance." You should have a comprehensive, adaptive plan that designs a better future based on your own definition of financial success and measured by specific benchmarks. "Fake it till you make it" is an artifact better off among the dinosaur bones. Our clients are intelligent, dynamic humans. Respect them and lead by example.

If you want to guide people's minds and habits toward more comprehensive financial planning, attempting to appeal to clients' egos will not work. We won't make clients feel like flashy rock stars with bragging rights for putting together a responsible plan for their future. While some turn to fear-based tactics, these typically only move the dial by tiny amounts—just enough to get you out of their hair.

We must instead build solid client relationships and earn our right to breach these unwelcome conversations because we've helped clients to see how they add genuine value. This is not an easy change to make. It requires that we don't settle for mediocrity, but rather work to unlock the formula that makes us truly trusted advisors. We also need to stop "serving" clients by fulfilling their one-off, transactional requests and shift to a model of truly *guiding* clients toward a more comprehensive long view of financial health. Our ability to evolve and mature as financial advisors will pay dividends for our clients—helping our own professional trajectories soar.

Cultivate Relationships and Create Value

New advisors sometimes try to approach financial sales similar to how they'd treat other "needs-and-desires" sales. Think of the Wall Street stockbroker appealing to ego—if a client wants a race car, just tie your penny stock to that outcome. As financial advisors, we soon learn that life insurance products don't easily lend themselves to ego sales, so, instead, many in our industry swap the ego-based model for a fear-based one—emphasizing what horrors may befall our clients if they don't invest in our products.

Admittedly, it *can* work to paint a picture of future risk (especially if you're convincing and charismatic), but it can also turn people off. These days, people have much more access to information—and misinformation. The outcome of having all the world's data, claims, opinions, and advice at our fingertips is that clients are less likely to put much stock into one solitary advisor's fear-based sales tactics. They may instead find them sensationalistic and manipulative, eroding their trust in you.

If we want to see positive change in our clients, we have to make some dramatic changes ourselves. Rather than clinging to outdated ego- and fear-based sales, let's instead broaden the lens of what's possible for our client using genuine *value creation*. Let's recognize that one transaction just marks the first step toward building a long-term relationship based in trust.

It's interesting to consider the difference between an advisor's perspective and a client's perspective after solving a specific isolated problem, maybe even the very problem the client came in the door looking for help with. At that moment in time, for the advisor, it is common to feel that they have reached the end of the sales process, and the deal is closed. There is nothing left to do. For the client, however, the conclusion of that transaction reflects the first time they have done business with you and, therefore, in their perspective the beginning of the relationship. When we only give clients what they ask for, we might solve a specific, isolated problem, which is not a bad thing in itself—as long as we also show clients the bigger picture of what's possible. As long as we recognize that we have reached level one of a relationship, and there is much more to be done. But how?

I often get pushback when I urge advisors with clients requesting specific products to slow down, take the time to prepare, and figure out the best they can do. Advisors ask me all the time, "If somebody wants to buy a product, why can't I just sell the product?"

My short (admittedly smart-ass) answer is, "You absolutely could, if your goal is to be a mediocre advisor. But if you know that you could have done better—that, in fact, you *would* have done better for yourself or a loved one—then you're basically telling the client, *I don't care about you*. Are you willing to say that out loud?"

This leads directly back to why our public opinion is so terrible. Because in only giving the client what they asked for, you may have answered a question accurately, but you didn't answer completely. Clients only see part of the picture, and it's our job to show them how different products and strategies fit into the overall plan, among the universe of options out there. We have expertise and experience our clients lack, and we know what impact partial answers can have on people. We have to show them the lost potential from a partial choice, versus the full compound impact of doing the whole job.

Finally, get away from averages and probabilities and focus on human data. We need to help people put themselves in the best possible situations financially. It may be true that only 1 percent of term insurance policies pay claims,[12] but that doesn't help families in that 1 percent if they don't own a policy. Maybe they heard a celebrity say they will get 12 percent portfolio growth each year,[13] ignoring the retiree living

---

[12] Ashlyn Brooks, "Term life insurance," Bankrate, June 24, 2024, https://www.bankrate.com/insurance/life-insurance/term-life-insurance/#what.

[13] Ramsey, "Can You Really Get a 12% Return on Your Investments?," RamseySolutions.com, July 3, 2024, https://www.ramseysolutions.com/retirement/the-12-reality.

through down markets that statistically come three years out of every ten.[14]

Instead of throwing numbers at people, we need to paint pictures of the future that compare likely "future-by-default" scenarios with their optimal vision of financial success. It's one thing to be able to scrape by because, based on past inaction, you now have no other choice. It's quite another thing to enjoy the compound impact of proper planning. Help clients see that generational wealth doesn't come from thinking about today; it comes from having vision.

Ask yourself, "Am I a visionary? Can I help my clients to become visionaries in their own lives?"

Of course, clients may take these robust plans one step at a time, and that's okay. We cannot force anyone to act on everything in an instant; we can only provide the full picture. Nor can we achieve perfection as advisors, but we can strive to be students of the business. We can aim to improve a bit every day, both at deepening relationships and trust and at motivating people to act more expediently than they might have without us. Not because their ego will "miss out" or because future uncertainty is scary but because they came to us to add value—to get further than they could without us. Let's at least give them a fighting chance.

---

[14] "10 Things You Should Know About Bear Markets," HartfordFunds.com, https://www.hartfordfunds.com/practice-management/client-conversations/managing-volatility/bear-markets.html#:~:text=Bear%20markets%20tend%20to%20be,average%20frequency%20between%20bear%20markets.

Patience Is Power

Sometimes, advisors resist broadening the lens to avoid seeming rude, pushy, or money grubbing. Other times, they tell me they were worried it would take too long to gather the information and paint that bigger picture. They figured if they didn't act now, they might lose an easy sale.

Here's where we see whether or not an advisor has truly made the change from a self-focused sales mentality to an others-focused mindset of impact-driven financial guidance. That's not to shame anyone, but rather to encourage introspection. If you notice you're worried about either being pushy or, on the flip side, taking too long and losing a sale, take that as helpful internal feedback. If you have established value at every step of the relationship, wouldn't your clients give you time to get to the punch line?

As soon as you give into the fear that you'll lose a sale for taking too long, you are thinking about yourself. Ironically, you've also seriously limited yourself because in not prioritizing a more comprehensive approach, you basically guarantee a lower future impact for everyone involved. This means you'll close a smaller sale, you'll be less important in their lives, and you'll be less "sticky" for this client. They'll engage with you less and take a limited view of your worth in terms of how knowledgeable you are and how much value your advice can offer them. All of this translates into fewer interactions and transactions with them—not to mention, fewer referrals and a smaller community impact.

As an advisor, hanging your ears on the bell means centering your clients' perspective and gathering as much information as you can. Then, and only then, should you recommend value-adding products and solutions directly relevant to your clients' goals and dreams.

When you look at it that way, the client-centered approach may seem like a no-brainer. But again, we humans tend to resist change and cling to our biases and blind spots. Many advisors expect clients to go from zero to one hundred, taking sudden, long-term action based on some quick and slick sales pitch, complete with a mind-bogglingly detailed spreadsheet. The reality is that every client relationship has its own cadence. While we can work to find those quick-thinking clients who shoot from the hip, there's also real value in respecting and working with slower-paced decision makers.

Advisors and leaders alike should reconsider the idea that if they just run faster, see more people, and get more signatures, then they will outperform. As a runner—albeit a very slow, poor runner—I read a lot of advice about training for distance and speed. They all say the same thing: To improve speeds overall, you have to learn to start slower and pace yourself.

Too often, we give advice through a narrow lens of competition and speed, comparing our metrics to those of other advisors and disparaging others' results rather than simply working toward maximum value creation for the client. We seem to think that our value comes through small details, as evidenced when we say, "Our rates of return will exceed those of this other firm," or, "The construction of this policy will outperform the one you currently own."

This approach reinforces public opinion that advisors are working against their clients' interests—even as you try to convince them you're swooping in to save the day. Our clients don't want a false financial messiah (they already have influencers for that). They need someone with vision. Someone to illustrate what's possible. To let them see the total potential—something more inspiring than replacing one transaction with one that is substantially the same.

I don't mean to diminish what it takes to get started in this career. I won't downplay the challenge of working in an industry that predominantly rewards advisors' results in terms of immediate sales in relatively short time frames, without much regard for impact data (rates of savings, referrals, etc.) and the leading indicators of a very successful career. Just as clients don't build their optimal financial futures overnight, it takes time for advisors to build lifelong client relationships and robust professional networks. But as we'll see in part five, that's where the real value and impact lies.

When getting into this career, make sure you can take the long view yourself. That might mean waiting until you have the financial resources and support system to ensure you won't have any internal conflicts when deciding between doing what is right and doing what is fast. If you're not ready, you're not ready. There is nothing to be ashamed of in that. You can always get a foot in the door while you build your foundation. One of the most impressive leaders I've met in our business is a woman who started out in this career as an assistant before rising to lead one of the most successful firms in the country.

Again, *it's not about you*. It's also not about other advisors or firms (sorry to say, your focus on competition with others is about you too). Rather, it's about the client and your value creation for that client.

Change Your Focus—and Your Habits

It's hard to change old habits, even when we know we should. I get why. In finance and sales—at work in general—we're trained to track our results and compete with others. To pursue rewards and avoid punishments. We easily get in the habit of setting goals based on outcomes like sales goals, earnings, and rankings. It's shortsighted and counterproductive.

Don't get me wrong, I am a HUGE fan of metrics. I'm not asking you to stop tracking progress; I'm asking you to use new metrics. Remember that former coach I mentioned who asked whether it was "possible, probable, or certain" that we'd reach our goals? The point is that success becomes more certain—or at least probable—when you base goals on client impact.

If we continue to chase self-focused metrics like earnings, sales, rankings, and AUM "takeovers," we perpetuate the old ways. Shift your focus to metrics like families helped, protections placed, systematic savings added, plans implemented, and relationships built, and your habits and outcomes will follow suit.

While chatting with my mother about this idea of rankings, I learned something interesting. When my siblings and I were growing up, she never rewarded or made a fuss over our class rankings at school. She argued that rankings didn't represent our own achievements. I could rank higher because I did better, but I also could rank higher because others did worse. Instead, she focused on whether or not we'd improved based on where we'd started and what goals we'd set. I guess her approach influenced my own—more than I knew—because to me, that's also the most meaningful measure of growth in our field, for advisors and clients both.

In particular, we should measure our own effectiveness as advisors based on the progress that's most impactful for our clients. To be sure, a well-managed large portfolio can lead to compound impact as well. Advisors can help wealthy clients multiply their legacy, helping them put structures in place to protect families, businesses, employees, and communities. But shuffling funds around is not the only value creation. Similarly impactful is helping a new homeowner protect their first major investment and begin to build toward the next.

In some careers, like sports, there's a clear mandate to win for winning's sake—for your team and/or yourself. You're certainly not trying to help the other team win the championship. However, in our business, our wins reflect the achievements of our clients—beyond what we achieve personally.

What does it say when we talk about inheriting someone's portfolio as "winning the client"? What have we won? Simply gaining a new account is not a measure of impact—it just means you convinced someone you might do a marginally better job. The real impact can only be measured in terms of comprehensive financial guidance over the long term.

We're not competitive athletes, and other advisors don't need to lose for us to "win." Don't worry about convincing clients that their previous advisor failed in some way or nitpicking about how you can improve on what they have done. The majority of advisors do a perfectly adequate job of constructing and managing portfolios.

This often surprises new advisors, but the figures I'm interested in relate to *adding* value, not gaining or inheriting it and not in comparing it to others. Let's focus more on where clients want to be and how we can help them progress toward those goals. The decisions a client has made so far in their lives—how much they're "worth"—may help us understand where to go next, but they tell us nothing about how our guidance will best impact their future. To figure that out, we need to actually bring advice to the table beyond what they already have implemented—not just an incrementally better portfolio construction or short-term product sales but something that will truly enhance their well-being in the future. If we can't do that, do we really deserve the client?

This others-focused concept isn't difficult to intellectually understand, but it takes time and practice to internalize and put into action. Plus, it can feel threatening to the ego. Just think about that self-interested fear of "losing the easy sale" by taking the time to focus on broader, longer-term value creation.

When we shift to a new profession or train a new skill, we sometimes make it about ourselves, not because we're megalomaniacs but simply because we're nervous. We want to prove ourselves, to compete for approval, to feel sure that we're doing a good job. It's perfectly healthy to look for this outside validation and feedback—to a point. In any field, we need to get over ourselves and widen our lens. In our case, that means focusing on authentic client impact, designing a plan, and then tracking those leading activity metrics to get to success.

Performing versus Engaging

Advisors often come out of meetings telling me, "That went great!"—only to never hear from the clients again. Why? Because they spent the meeting in performance mode, unknowingly detached from the client's perspective. They got stuck in their own heads and in their own spiels—and in so doing, they got it wrong. Next, they start theorizing about why the clients didn't want to transact with them. Or they just throw their hands up and say, "I don't know."

My response is always, "Well, the easiest way to find out would be to ask them. If you care about clients getting the best for themselves, it should be easy to reach out and say, 'Hey, thanks for coming in! To help me bring more value to people, I was wondering if you could share why you decided not to work with me at this time.'"

Advisors generally don't like to ask for feedback, especially when they suspect deep down that they were not being authentic. What I'd like advisors to understand is the extent to which we get to be real human beings at work. In fact, that might be the single best way to add value for our clients, ourselves, and our firms. (You may also find that learning to be vulnerable turns out to be the best way to end up with that Ferrari.)

Speaking with a client should not feel performative. You don't need to mentally evaluate how "good of a job" you're doing as you're doing it. Instead, try to inhabit the perspective of the client. This pulls in soft skills like patience, communication, and empathy. Don't worry about what clients think of you or whether or not the conversation will end with a sale. Worry about whether or not they are *with you*. Consider where the client is at every stage in the process. The change we need to make starts with meeting them where they are. Then, we can move forward with them, one step at a time. That's what it means to be a trusted advisor.

In a gender workshop I attended years ago, the moderator explained that, in general, men nod their heads when they agree with what's being said. Women, however, tend to nod simply to show they're following what you're saying. Understanding subtle cues like this can help you when asking direct questions about important matters. *Does this make sense? Do you agree? Do you want to take action to improve this situation?*

If you keep the focus on yourself, your confidence will remain conditional on whether or not people "like" you or make a fast purchase. You'll tend to jump ahead in fear of getting a "no." But when you instead put the focus on the other people, it changes everything. Not only does it help you better understand both their current situation and their vision for the future, but it also roots your confidence in something more stable—namely, in guiding that person to the best advice for the best possible outcome. (The rest is up to them.)

Many new advisors assume they need to look like experts who know everything or like top-of-the-field competitors who outperform everyone else. They conspicuously display their own success in hopes that driving a fast car and showing off a wall of sales trophies will convince clients to work with them. That mentality reflects the same misconceptions as the woman who ravaged her credit to bring a Louis Vuitton bag to job interviews. The reality is that such overt expressions of power often serve to widen the chasm between the person talking and the person listening. I'm not saying you can't have nice things—that is, if you have earned them and can afford them. I am, however, saying that it will not help you to have nice things when you haven't earned them or can't afford them.

Clients do care about our ability—our competence, our experience, and our compatibility with them. They do not necessarily care how our sales metrics compare to the person in the office next door. They want to know that we understand their unique needs and goals, that we're a good personal fit, and that we're willing to take the time to customize the right approach for them. We do this by asking questions, not by showing off how much we know. It may sound cliché, but that Maya Angelou quote put it best: "People will forget what you said, people will forget what you did, but people will never forget how you made them feel."

Humans may be wired to seek short-term rewards (spending) over long-term benefits (insurance products, retirement savings, etc.), but they do actually care about their resources and their futures. They want to walk away feeling like you, as their advisor, listened to them and took genuine interest in their priorities, concerns, and goals. This isn't like the restaurant waiter vying for a good tip. Our work goes far beyond short-term service. Ideally, it extends through the rest of our clients' lives, and maybe even beyond them.

Here's an example. For the advisor who's really interested in finance, it may seem like the most important thing to all clients is their rate of return on investments. If you operate only through this lens, you'll only have success with some clients—the ones focused on higher-risk, one-dimensional gains—not with everyone. And, whether or not that client can see it now, the compound impact of joining them in that narrow lens will hurt them more than it will help you.

If you meet with a couple who say they're scared about running out of money during retirement and all you do is talk about maximizing their rate of return, you've totally missed the point.

We're not here to prescribe solutions based on what we feel people should do with their money. Instead, we need to focus on what the clients themselves want in the future, what *they* value, and what outcomes they ultimately define as successful. Then, it's our job to recommend opportunities and products that offer the best path forward, while always asking permission to bring up areas they may have missed.

Beyond Band-Aid Advising

Let's say someone goes to the doctor with a headache. The fact that they took the trouble to make the appointment and show up suggests they've passed the self-medication phase. No physician would recommend the most obvious over-the-counter pain medicine without first asking additional questions and screening them for more serious issues, like a stroke or meningitis. We would cry malpractice if a doctor failed to look at the big picture when it comes to our physical health, so why has it become so commonplace in our profession?

Why wouldn't we cultivate a similar culture when looking after people's financial health? Let's say a client reaches out with a specific concern. They might say, "I'm really worried about how this election is going to impact my portfolio." A knee-jerk response would be to cite some statistics about past election cycles and, at most, offer to reallocate their portfolio, if they insist.

To truly add value, we need to operate like detectives. We need to dig deeper and gather more information by asking, "*Why* are you worried about that?" and "When do you expect to use this money?" If you haven't already done so, it might be the ideal time to schedule a review to show them a projection for the future. How much money is at risk in the market, and how much is not? What sort of income generation do we expect in the future, and are there any risks we haven't considered that should be addressed? Is there anything that may prompt you to sell out of your portfolio in the near future to generate liquidity? The real risks our clients face are generally not tied to the news headlines of the day.

The grand change I envision starts small. I ask that you simply dial it in by doing a little better every day. A trusted advisor is someone who has been given a seat at the client's table. You are not there to simply answer the direct questions they asked but to take on the roles and responsibilities of a strategic guide who can see around corners. There's immense untapped opportunity, not just in the clients you have not met yet but also in the clients you haven't fully helped yet. The projected retirement shortfall in this country falls somewhere between 6.8 and 14 trillion dollars.[15] I'd say that math sounds a bit conservative, but whatever the number, some of those people already have financial advisors. I hope they aren't your clients.

Too many advisors take an obvious, Band-Aid approach. Maybe they say, "Let's make your investments more conservative by adjusting the risk tolerance." That may also be a good option, but unless you can broaden the lens to examine the root concern and consider all the risks and opportunities, you won't maximize client impact.

You can build a career as a reactive, Band-Aid advisor, but you'll be replaced sooner or later. This only limits your own progress, as well as your impact on others. This does a disservice

---

[15] Nari Rhee, "The Retirement Savings Crisis: Is It Worse Than We Think?," National Institute on Retirement Security, June 2013, https://www.nirsonline.org/reports/the-retirement-savings-crisis-is-it-worse-than-we-think/#:~:text=The%20collective%20retirement%20savings%20gap,on%20working%20until%20age%2067.

to clients and consumers, as well as to yourself, your firm, and our industry as a whole. Whether or not you see it right away, Band-Aids have a negative compound impact on your career.

Be the Change

People naturally resist change, so we need to cultivate patience and keep the focus where it should be: on compound impact. That's not always easy to do, given the natural human tendency to privilege short-term rewards over potential long-term benefits, and this goes for both our clients and for ourselves. The same impulse that drives clients to overspend, take on risky loans, and make bad financial decisions (even when they know they are doing it) also drives advisors to the same shortfalls.

When we hyper-focus on returns and sales, we operate out of ego or fear. It's not easy to become aware of such habits, let alone change them, but that's exactly what our industry needs. There are literally millions of Americans who could benefit from our help, if we could just better model the behaviors we want to see in our clients and learn to sit on their side of the table as their advisors.

Our current practices prevent ordinary people from getting the full help they need and enjoying the best possible outcomes. Our reluctance to work with families, neighbors, and friends limits our impact, as does our industry's insistence on perpetuating the notion that only the wealthy seek out our help. These practices make people feel like we cannot help them. The resulting delay in seeking our help limits the number of Americans building true generational wealth. Finally, these behaviors perpetuate advisor burnout from the self-imposed expectations and the resulting treadmill of constantly chasing after new clients.

If we want to change our clients' perspectives—not to mention our industry's reputation—we must change how we operate. It's essential that we get out of our own heads, sit on the same side of the table as our clients, make sure our clients feel heard and understood, and then help them see the full, magnificent picture of what is possible together.

GUT CHECK

When did I exhibit patience this week?

Where is my true focus? On what I would do in the client's shoes? Or somewhere else?

Did my clients react as I expected? If not, was I "performing" my worth rather than centering the clients' perspectives in the first place?

Did I recognize and avoid isolated "Band-Aid" solutions in favor of longer-term, integrated strategies that will yield better compound impact?

CHAPTER 8

CHANGE *for* LEADERS

As leaders in our field, are we happy with where we are? Do we want to keep going as we have, or do we want to lead a change? To put it in a way that mirrors our most essential question to clients: Do we want to keep the status quo and risk our future by default—or take action to ensure a future by design?

Right now, the future by default looks like a self-perpetuating negative feedback loop. We struggle to recruit enough qualified candidates (often based on narrow, outdated, or misaligned requirements). We fail to retain those we recruit for more than a few years (often based on narrow, outdated, or misaligned development).

General public mistrust compounds the problem, as our industry's poor reputation turns people off. This includes those genuinely others-focused professionals driven by purpose and impact, whom we desperately need in the profession. Meanwhile, government regulations actively further undermine client trust, while deterring people who care about people from considering our field. If such professionals do end up in the business, our training and development models reinforce the old, competitive, sales-based tactics, causing disillusionment and burnout.

If we try to combat this spiral in an argumentative, defensive way, we're not going to change anything. I find it can backfire to go in with guns blazing, aggressively trying to change people's minds. This only prompts counter defenses and reinforces negative loops. Instead, I want to acknowledge the immense good our profession has done over the decades. In 2023 alone, life insurance benefits and claims paid out in the United States exceeded $830 billion. Thirty-seven percent of Americans—roughly 123 million people—had financial advisors.[16] In fact, that's exactly why I work hard to push for change, out of a deep respect and appreciation for the work we do and how it can change lives. We don't have to lose sight of our many successes in our efforts to make changes that increase our positive impact.

Globally, the world looks to the United States as leaders in our field. That's partly because the US accounts for 59 percent of all global stock market capitalization[17] and 58 percent of the global insurance market.[18] When I've accepted invitations to speak internationally, audiences inevitably want to know how advisors in the US operate within our mature market.

---

[16] "Two-Thirds of Americans Say Their Financial Planning Needs Improvement," Northwestern Mutual, July 24, 2023, https://news.northwesternmutual.com/2023-07-24-Two-Thirds-of-Americans-Say-Their-Financial-Planning-Needs-Improvement.

[17] "Two-Thirds of Americans Say Their Financial Planning Needs Improvement."

[18] Jennifer Rudden, "Market share of the total insurance market worldwide from 2000 to 2022, by country," Statista, June 31, 2024, https://www.statista.com/statistics/1045207/market-share-of-insurance-worldwide-by-country/#:~:text=Between%202000%20and%202022%2C%20the,of%20more%20than%2080%20percent.

They want to know how they can emulate us. I always reply that while they should learn from our achievements, they'd also be wise to skip our mistakes. We'd all benefit from more focus on impact.

As with clients, we can only change course with advisors and other leaders by meeting them where they are, then offering appropriate guidance from there. We need to study why clients don't trust us, why the government keeps trying to regulate our work, and why impact-driven professionals who excel at building relationships hesitate to enter our field. This relates to how we attract, recruit, and retain both advisors and leaders, as well as how we train, develop, and reinforce the impact-driven mindset rather than solely focusing on transactional metrics. There's no doubt that we did get to where we are today through a heavy focus on transactions. But the world has changed, and our clients expect much more from us now. We have to continue to work as hard as we always have, just with a different focus.

We can't create an others-focused, impact-driven industry with self-interested approaches. In competing over limited sales talent already in our field and rewarding our people based solely on who advises the wealthiest clients or sells the most products, we focus on our own ego- and fear-based interests, not on our client impact. This detracts from our potential to help close the retirement savings gap (currently in the trillions) and create multigenerational impact for both our clients and our profession.

It's time to design a better future for our field by acknowledging—and fundamentally changing—unhelpful patterns in the way that we attract, recruit, train, and support advisors.

Attracting and Recruiting

We naturally attract a lot of people who went to finance school. These candidates like to talk about their successes in building strong investment portfolios. They provide metrics demonstrating how they ranked academically among their cohort and how steep the competition ran.

Now, I appreciate market savvy as much as the next financial leader. I still remember an anecdote a candidate once shared during an interview about a class project. The assignment was to build a model portfolio. At the end of the semester, the students convened to see who had "realized" the most wealth. In a brilliant (and quite hilarious) move, the professor awarded the prize to the only student who remembered to sell out of the model portfolio, pointing out that shares were not *realized* wealth until they were sold.

Great lessons like this will serve any financial advisor. But market savvy is only one part of the picture. While a finance background helps reduce the learning curve for new advisors, those technical skills are easier to teach than the others-centered soft skills required to truly become a trusted advisor. Advisors don't spend their careers in back offices staring at spreadsheets all day; we're primarily building trusted, long-term relationships. And yes, we need to understand complex financial structures and crunch numbers, but we pay equal attention to the human data. (At least if we want to be effective, we do.)

Part of the challenge relates to how colleges and universities currently train aspiring advisors for our industry. While they provide some focus on "behavioral finance," which delves into how people react to market information (usually to the detriment of their portfolios), that's just the tip of the iceberg. To understand how to be effective financial advisors, students need training in interpersonal communication, social work, marketing, and business, for a start. They need to understand the great responsibility they have and the social consequences of mediocre advice.

Reflecting Our Communities

Again, I'm not saying that you shouldn't recruit finance or salespeople, just asking, why not also target a broader audience in your hiring campaigns? If we're looking to serve all our communities effectively, it helps to have a diverse range of backgrounds among our ranks. People with experience in hospitality or the supply chain business will better serve clients in those related fields, for example. When describing the ideal candidate in job postings, we also have the opportunity to emphasize the crucial soft skills needed to thrive in a field based on relationship building: listening, communicating, collaborating as a team or partner, meeting people where they are, and guiding clients toward a better outcome. We must find that somewhat elusive mix of self-motivation combined with a focus on impact to others.

Finally, we can include a focus on encouraging women and minorities who feel they'd be a good fit to apply even when they don't meet every listed requirement. *Harvard Business Review* reports that, when looking at a job description and seeing that long laundry list of the skills and qualifications needed for the job, men (especially white men) tend to apply to jobs of interest even if they can only check off most requirements—about 60 percent.[19] Women and people from less traditional or advantaged backgrounds, meanwhile, typically won't apply unless they're 100 percent qualified. It won't be possible to mirror our local communities if we can't attract a much more diverse population to the career in the first place. Notice the demographics next time you're out running errands or attending a community event—does your team reflect what you see? Suit up for the future, because it's already here.

This isn't *Mary Poppins*. It's a fantasy to imagine that we'll manage to always find the perfect candidate who magically checks every box and truly understands how to make an impact in our business. Even more ridiculous is to imagine that the only way to build a successful team is to recruit and train an army of clones trained for the 1950s. Our current retention rates and public reputation suggest a serious disconnect between the people who think this is the career for them and those who will truly thrive in it. If we don't change how we approach sourcing, we're positioning ourselves to play reruns of the same irrelevant, outdated show.

I can't tell you how much I've learned from our firm's diverse team of advisors. In my experience, companies thrive best when their people complement each other's strengths, from analysis and sales, to creativity and interpersonal skills. But while I'm proud of the gains we've made, I'm not naive to the fact that we've barely scratched the surface. It's not enough to simply *look* diverse at the advisor level. We must also get

---

[19] Tara Sophia Mohr, "Why Women Don't Apply for Jobs Unless They're 100% Qualified," *Harvard Business Review*, August 25, 2014, https://hbr.org/2014/08/why-women-dont-apply-for-jobs-unless-theyre-100-qualified.

to the point where our leaderboards and awards ceremonies (rewarding the right things, of course) also reflect that diversity.

One of the most impactful comments I've heard regarding diversity came from Ursula Burns, the first Black woman to lead an S&P 500 company. During a CNN interview in the wake of the 2020 "Black Lives Matters" protests, she spoke about the challenges African Americans face, asking, "Don't you think if we had the answers, we would have already fixed this?" This question emphasizes that the problems we face need across-the-aisle solutions involving multiple (good-faith) perspectives.

Finally, when recruiting for diversity, make sure you know why you're doing it. Are you just trying to cynically hit some arbitrary quota to look good? Or do you care about increasing your impact on communities through better representation? I value diversity because I've seen the innovative outcomes, collaborative spirit, and compound impact you get when your team boasts a variety of skills, perspectives, and backgrounds. The potential is unknown, and untapped, because we have not fully invested in it.

"Vetting" Candidates

It's good to check credentials and hold candidates to high standards overall, but let's critically examine how we do that—and how good we are at it. Do we even know what we should be "vetting" for?

When interviewing, I mainly focus on matters related to drive/motivation, trust, and engagement. Are candidates more driven by sales and personal gain? Or do they aspire to grow as individuals through having a positive impact on their clients and communities? Can they describe a time when they successfully built or repaired trust at work? How comfortable would they feel working with friends and family? What are some ways they engage with their communities and develop their professional networks? Are they willing to compromise what is right for the sake of a sale, or will they hold their ground and do the right thing?

Beyond the specific questions you ask, notice how candidates interact with you during interviews. I'm not just talking about how outgoing and charismatic they are. (Speaking of diversity, some of our most effective and impressive advisors are true introverts.)

Focus instead on how well they listen. How engaged do they seem? Do they cut you off and overemphasize their numeric achievements or show off their knowledge of facts and figures? Do they have the ability to read the room? Can they genuinely connect with other people? Did they learn anything about you, and did you learn anything about them? Did you find a way to relate to each other?

On the theme of part four, you should also screen for how well candidates can change and adapt. How well do they take outside feedback? You don't want to hire someone based on their hotshot metrics only to discover that they take even simple, gentle critiques super personally. There is no longer any room in this business for compliance risks or for people who like to "paint outside of the lines" when it comes to ethics.

This brings us to another great test of how self- versus others-focused someone is—just ask some critical questions or offer a contrasting view of something they say during the interview. Note whether they contract into a defensive state or get curious about and energized by your feedback or argument. All financial advisors experience adversity and pushback from clients, so make sure they can handle it with grace.

Financial advisors are leaders in their communities. They are confident, independent, and, yes, generally opinionated. As leaders, we have to be able to tell the difference between a leader who will have followers and a leader who is a lone wolf. It's a fine line sometimes.

In this field, we must learn from mistakes and criticism. Advisors and leaders both need the resilience, innovation, and humility of a growth mentality. We need to get curious and constantly learn and adapt in our constant push toward better results.

The Limits of Expertise

Many new and aspiring advisors assume they have to know everything before they begin. They believe that clients look to them as they would to a Google search. We reflect this misconception as leaders when we dump tons of information on them, as though that technical knowledge is going to make them great advisors.

The job of an advisor is to attract a prospective client to the table, uncover their goals, and then synthesize information into a customized plan. To do that, we don't need to know everything in advance. In fact, we *can't* know all the answers before we've fully examined the questions. If you ever played with a piñata as a child, you know the image of a blindfolded person, dizzy from spinning around, wildly swinging in the air with a bat. That's the image my mind conjures up when I see an inexperienced advisor spewing answers without properly listening or orienting themselves to their clients. They're already trying to solve problems before even knowing which way is up.

Besides, by the time advisors have done all the training and read all the books to get the licenses and credits and letters after their names, everything's already changing—the regulations, the products, the whole environment. We do need relevant technical knowledge about solutions and strategies we recommend, but the answers change and evolve along with our technology and consumer needs, and knowledge itself is not what makes a great advisor. It's our job to make sure they have the resources to get and deliver all the information needed, but most importantly we must first teach them how to earn their clients' trust.

Training with an Others-Focused Approach

Our advisors need to understand where our clients are coming from and how to get them where they want to go. That comes from training them in the art of interpersonal skills: communicating, asking the right questions, and listening to learn how clients feel about things and what they want. Only then should advisors use that client-centered human data to imagine and execute the most amazing outcomes possible for their clients.

Another misconception among new advisors is that they will magically fit into a community they know nothing about just because of their knowledge—without even trying to understand, let alone *reflect*, that community's values or practices. I remember an inexperienced advisor seeking coaching from me. She explained that she and a senior advisor had scheduled an appointment with a partner at a law firm. When the three had sat down in the meeting, the lawyer had directed all his attention and questions to the senior advisor, a gentleman dressed in a traditional suit and tie.

This had left her feeling disrespected, so she asked my advice on how to respond. Noticing her outfit, I calmly asked, "You went into an attorney's office wearing a tank top that shows your tattoos and bright purple lipstick. Considering your audience, what type of attention were you expecting?" If you want to work in a community, you should genuinely care about being a part of it.

There's more than one way to make the wrong impression. In this case, the advisor passively conveyed disrespect for her client's community, without even saying a word. If our advisors want to command respect, it's our job to coach them to work with audiences in ways they can relate to (and vice versa). At the bare minimum, it helps to show up looking like you expected to have a business meeting.

On the other hand, we can't just hire a financial advisor and tell them they need to "look the part" and project a successful "abundance mindset" by going out and buying a sports car and designer clothes. If someone had convinced me to buy a Ferrari when I had just started out, I would have hidden in a closet and cried for fear of going bankrupt. That approach simply doesn't work for most people, including a lot of women and people from less advantaged backgrounds. I've interviewed advisors who pulled into the parking lot in a $100,000 car, and they're not yet making $30,000 a year. Looking the part does not magically lead to better outcomes. More often, it just leads to collections accounts and wrecked credit.

Becoming the center of your community, however, does work. To have a broader client and community impact, our advisors need to meet people—a lot of people. Not all at once but consistently over time, with an eye toward making and maintaining a positive impression. Ideally, they should become the center of a community they care about, relate to, and would be honored to serve.

When it comes to reputation and image, the smallest things will go a long way. Are you showing up on time? Are you volunteering and delivering on your promises? Are you sticking your neck out and offering to help people work out both big and small problems in their financial lives? Some of my most extensive and mutually profitable client relationships have been referred to me by individuals with much smaller accounts and more limited advising needs. Trust gets passed on by people's relationships and characters, not by the weight of their wallets.

Measuring Impact

To reinforce the others-centered approach, we have to measure and reward the right things. How many new clients has an advisor helped in the past year? Did the advisor help clients create a strategy for paying down credit card debt? Or, one of my personal favorites, how much have they helped clients increase their systematic savings?

If a client saves just 1 percent of their income when they come in, and your advisor helps them get up to 2, 5, or 20 percent, those incremental increases in savings over the client's lifetime will have a transformational impact on their future wealth. This, to me, is a powerful metric.

By now, it's probably clear that I'm not big on shortcuts. Combining a focus on impact with the deep trust earned by true engagement will get our advisors to success faster and more effectively than hoping someone picks up the phone on a cold call. Yes, this approach requires some faith and commitment, but it more than pays off. There are countless communities that need our help, and we have a responsibility to find, attract, train, and deliver advisors who are willing to engage.

If we truly want to have the greatest impact on clients, we have to measure and reinforce these efforts. If we can demonstrate how we consistently grow the security and long-term prosperity of our clients, it will change how clients interact with us and how the general public views us. We'll bring in a greater volume of clients with more loyalty, leading to longer-term, faster-growing accounts and more referrals. We'll retain more advisors who genuinely value their client relationships and know how to work as a team. Finally, we'll also have a greater impact on generational wealth among our communities, which can't help but shift public perception.

Finally, we need to develop both advisors and leaders. To do so, we need to measure candidates' ability to lead this kind of change. For example, if diversity is one of our goals, that doesn't mean just meeting a DEI quota and moving on. We need to empower those individuals (and all our hires) with the training and support needed to become top advisors and leaders. We should seek out feedback, show some humility in areas where none of us can claim to be experts, and work hard to move the needle. That's how we will begin to improve our retention of these advisors and how we will achieve a measurable impact within their communities.

Retention

If our advisors aren't succeeding or sticking around, we need to see that as feedback for our own leadership. Retention reflects on us—on how we recruit, train, and support our people. When we get that right, retention figures will naturally improve. It is not reasonable to select people through our personally designed process and then blame them for our failures. Our retention rates are reflections on us.

Instead of identifying and solving the underlying issues, many leaders tend to look at these abysmal retention rates and say, "We know we're going to lose people, so let's just find more of them." Think about the message that this sends to your newest advisors—the ones who are excited to be a part of the firm and willing to run through a brick wall to stay with you. How does it feel when, within a week of joining the firm, we ask them to introduce us to potential replacements? We can't blame them for thinking, *I just got here. You're already done with me?*

This attitude reflects the popular definition of insanity: doing the same things while expecting different results. This approach basically guarantees the poor retention rates that perpetuate our field's downward spiral. We can only grow advisors so much when we retain just 15 percent of them over a four-year period. We can't just coach our advisors on how to earn client referrals without also making this change as *leaders*. We can model how to make referrals about us: "Can you introduce me to anyone you know who might be interested in joining our field?" Or, we can model how to make it about others: "You mentioned some friends were excited to hear about our work culture. Should we invite any of them in to learn more about the firm and this career possibility?" Sometimes there's a fine line between others-focused and self-interested approaches, and we cannot lose sight of that as leaders.

Think about how much you could grow your firm's reach, impact, and revenue if you retained 70 to 80 percent of your advisors. Now, imagine how much we could reduce the trillions of dollars of deficit in retirement savings if more Americans had advisors focused on maximizing positive long-term impact. What if we could increase the proportion of Americans with advisors from 37 percent to 80 percent or more? If lobbyists and lawmakers understood this, we could focus on increasing access to comprehensive financial planning—not on restricting and complicating it further.

From Lone Wolf to Teamwork

We won't shift to a future by design unless we ask the right questions—and they're not always comfortable questions. Are we attracting the right people to the business? Are we developing and supporting them in the right ways? Are we rewarding the right skills and efforts?

This used to be more of a "lone wolf" business, glorifying the top advisor who racked up sales. Now, we're starting to see more of a team approach that values different skill sets and emphasizes collaboration. You could have an advisor who mainly focuses on business development and relationship building and another colleague who steps in to help execute those strategies. As leaders, we can honor each advisor's vision for their future in the business, while also being authentic and directly communicating what it takes to succeed in their role.

If someone wants to be a lead advisor, they must understand the required skills and commit to a plan of action to master them. While it's wonderful to crunch numbers and generate reports, that's more of an administrative function than a lead function. To be a lead advisor, you can have all of the skills or some of the skills, but the one that is essential is the ability to be a rainmaker. This business centers around people: collaborating with teams, working with colleagues, motivating people to meet with you, and inspiring clients to act—those are the real leadership skills.

It's not any one advisor's job to have all the answers, but rather to know where to get those answers. That means that the primary relationship manager may need to learn how to delegate, manage resources, and bring in other team members for matters outside their areas of expertise. This is not a pattern that the "lone wolf" advisors of the past embraced, but as the business has become more complicated, it is essential.

If advisors are truly thinking about the best outcomes for a client, they should seek other specialists or professionals when doing so could improve client outcomes. As leaders, we need to recognize that none of this can happen if we stay rooted in the structures and systems of the past. We'll never move the dial if we only reward competition and profits and seem to ignore professional collaboration and client impact.

These changes reflect a larger societal shift toward a more agile, interconnected, collaborative world. People have more options and information at their fingertips than ever before. They need guidance they can trust from engaged advisors who are motivated by the right things. As advisors and leaders, we're good at designing better futures for our advisors, but we can't get complacent; there's much more to be done. This may involve looking outside our ranks and learning from the most innovative companies on the planet. We need to balance the safety and security that our profession demands with the expectations our clients have for a modern experience. We're responsible for designing this better future for ourselves and for our industry as a whole.

That's certainly not to malign the entire industry. Our successes in the United States impress our colleagues around the world for a reason. It would be crazy not to respect and celebrate the icons of our profession—those incredible advisors and leaders who have built our field to where it is today. But it would be equally crazy to think that they were born that way. We won't have success hunting for fully developed advisors. This only leads to unreasonable expectations that exacerbate our attrition problems. Instead, we need to accept that it is our job to train and develop the people who will then become the next generation of icons. What are we doing to mentor and train them? Are we able to meet them where they are and guide them toward greater success? Or are we applying outdated methods and unreasonable standards?

Don't forget that many of our industry giants were recruited and developed in a different time. We live in a dynamic world that's constantly redefining how we professionally engage with and add value to each other's lives. Sometimes, our very notions of "success" or "leadership" need a refresh. We also can't immediately hold the next generation of advisors to the standards of icons with decades of experience, but should rather seek to develop those new to our field into strong advisors and leaders—in ways best suited to them, their clients, and their communities.

As our industry grapples with reputation, regulation, and retention issues, we're faced with a choice. We could plow ahead with the same old tactics—looking for advisors with demonstrated sales records, convincing them to switch to our firm, then promoting internal competition and rewarding transactions. But if we do, nothing will change.

GUT CHECK

Can our advisors tell the difference between a hypothetical portfolio and real life?

Are we serious about diversity—digging in and making progress?

Are we looking for client-centered candidates or vetting with our outdated assumptions?

How are we helping our advisors find their communities?

CHAPTER 9

IMPACT *for* ADVISORS

I once worked with a young mortgage broker ("Sam") whom I'd met in a structured business networking group. As a group, we got together weekly to support each other through education, business connections, and introductions.

Sam and I had known each other for years, and he'd heard me talk about insurance dozens of times before he reached out to me about a term life insurance policy. Specifically, he wanted me to send him the forms required to purchase a policy for $500,000.

Based on this client's income level—and the fact that he and his wife had three young children—I knew Sam should do much better for his family and that this number would be wholly inadequate, should they ever need it.

As you know, simply stating that would have gotten me nowhere. Clients live in absolutes, not averages. To them, the situation is clear: They either live or they die. Considering how few term insurance policies pay claims (only about 1 percent)—and the fact that the best-case scenario is that clients "waste their premium"—they can be a hard sell. However, it's our job to think about that 1 percent.

"Let's find a time to sit down and talk about it," I said. He replied that he was too busy to meet and again requested the paperwork, since he "already knew exactly what [he] wanted."

"How about this," I said. "Why don't I meet you and your wife this weekend, bring the paperwork, and we'll go over things together?"

Sam agreed. Since his wife, Rebecca, stayed home with their children, I drove out to their home as promised. During that visit, I recommended $6 million in life insurance for Sam and $3 million for Rebecca, which was the maximum amount of coverage they could obtain. I explained that those amounts would fully indemnify them against the potential loss of his income over his remaining working years or the potential loss of Rebecca as a primary caregiver for their children and chief of staff to the business of running their home and their lives. I shared my philosophy that it's my job to educate my clients on the very best they can do for themselves and their family by fully insuring their income the same way they would fully insure their homes.

No one expects their home to burn down, yet we all indemnify against that possibility, happy to "waste" our premiums without a second thought. Many people even take the time to fully insure their cell phones or wedding rings. Given that premature deaths have far more dire and lasting consequences, I feel it's part of my job to help clients give the matter due consideration.

After some deliberation, Sam and Rebecca chose to purchase $3 million for him and $1.5 million for her. This was less than I'd recommended (less than fully insured) but certainly far more than they'd been in the market for.

At that time, I believed I had done a good job. This visit was not about convincing a couple to buy more than they'd asked for, but rather to help them consider the purpose of the purchase, what they were insuring, and what it would look like to take complete action. In doing so, I helped this young couple go much further with my guidance than they could have without me.

About four years later, Sam passed away in a tragic car accident, when he and Rebecca were both in their mid-thirties. As soon as I heard the news, I drove out to visit Rebecca and the kids, helped answer their questions, and reassured them I was there for them as long as they needed me. The first thing she asked for help with was to accompany her to the funeral home to pick up the death certificates.

I think sometimes about the fact that if I had done what Sam had asked and sold him the $500,000 plan, I might never have met Rebecca.

I still would have helped her—to some extent. She might have used that money to help pay off the mortgage on their home. After doing so, she still would have faced nearly $20,000 a year in real estate taxes alone, not to mention the cost of utilities, repairs, and landscaping, and that's just the cost of their home. Factor in vehicles, health insurance, medical bills, childcare, school expenses, extracurriculars—the list goes on and on. Surviving with a paid-off home but no income would not have been sustainable for long.

Long story short, Rebecca's life—and those of her kids—would have turned upside down and inside out overnight, as she dramatically and urgently downsized their lives. Sam's death would have forced her to go back to work in her much lower paid field of early childhood education after years out of the workforce. This would require paid childcare for the younger children and moving their older child out of private school and into a public system. Finally, Rebecca almost certainly would have had to sell their home and move to a more affordable neighborhood or back to family support several states away, uprooting her children and their lives in another destabilizing change.

All of a sudden, their children would have been grieving not only their father but also the only home, community, and lifestyle they'd ever known. When you look at the material and emotional implications, it's clear that most of the transactions we make as financial advisors are not about money; they're about reducing harm and negative impact, while setting clients and their families up for long-term security and success.

Now, more than a decade later, Rebecca and her children are still in their same family home. They have continued their lives, and they are still grieving their loss. Absolutely no dollar amount can ever replace the loss of a loved one. The most our profession can offer is material security combined with an advisor's emotional support, but that's no small thing when everything else is falling apart.

Client-centered, impact-driven financial guidance means putting people in the optimal position they can be in. To help them and their family live better, which benefits communities and subsequent generations to come. We do that by taking the time to really get to know our clients and building a strategy based on their unique situation and goals—one aimed at reducing harm, optimizing positive impact, and cementing legacy.

I couldn't see the future when I first met this family, and I can't see the future today. None of us can. But what we *can* do is develop and implement plans that work for people. We can protect lifestyles and help ensure both upward mobility and generational wealth. That is what I mean by compound impact.

The Cost of Partial Action

I have worked with and trained hundreds of advisors, interviewed thousands, and spoken in front of thousands more. The truth is that in all my years in the business, I have never once personally witnessed an advisor causing harm to clients. What I *have* seen is that most advisors, most of the time, fall short of the potential impact they can have on their clients and communities.

In thinking about the sale rather than its impact, advisors and clients both miss the forest for the trees. Sadly, our society encourages and even rewards this. We're urged to go with the minimum required insurance and savings plans. Meanwhile, we're told it's in our best interests to go with higher-risk investments. If you ask me, it's in all clients' best interests to do the opposite, opting for the maximum protection, maximum savings, and mitigated risks. There's a time and a place for chasing higher yield opportunities, but for me, that's never before the foundation is firmly in place.

The vast majority of advisors would have simply given Sam what he'd asked for and called it a win. To me, that's not advising. Rather it's a reactive, transactional approach focused on pleasing the client and closing a short-term sale. It's time to start measuring impact in terms of opportunity costs and potential optimal impact. While you can certainly argue that the $500,000 isn't a bad thing, how does passing up millions of dollars in potential benefits really help clients? Are we not, at the very least, responsible for bringing the idea to the table?

It's more difficult to help our clients achieve their best possible outcomes when the public views us as mercenaries out for our own gain. But after about two decades in this business, I can confidently say that I've never witnessed any truly mercenary behavior in any financial advising company or environment. There are a lot of practices I don't agree with, but at the end of the day, there's truly not much damage done in the act of selling insurance policies or reallocating investment portfolios. Instead, the problem I see relates to the unfortunate ripple effects of unfulfilled potential—for both the advisors and the clients—by not doing a more complete job.

What is the real potential here? The potential impact of improving our reputations and changing public perception? Almost half of Americans don't have any life insurance, even though 30 percent recognize that they need it.[20] Nearly 8,000 people die in the United States *every day*, which means somewhere in the neighborhood of 4,000 do so without any life insurance.[21]

---

[20] Jennifer Lobb and Heidi Gollub, "Life insurance statistics and industry trends 2024," *USA Today*, January 24, 2024, https://www.usatoday.com/money/blueprint/life-insurance/life-insurance-statistics/#:~:text=This%20is%20according%20to%20the,don't%20have%20it%20yet.

[21] Statista Research Department, "Daily number of coronavirus (COVID-19) deaths compared to influenza and all causes in the United States as of January 6, 2022," Statista, July 27, 2022, https://www.statista.com/statistics/1109281/covid-19-daily-deaths-compared-to-all-causes/#:~:.

It's on our shoulders to take real accountability for how others perceive us—and do a better job. That means getting away from a model of taking orders from clients for isolated Band-Aid solutions and instead looking for opportunities for greater impact. We need to get away from negative concepts like "cross-selling" and "upselling" and move toward closing the gap between where clients are today and their optimal "future by design." We don't want our clients to retire in austerity with the bare minimum security, but rather to thrive amid the best possible outcomes.

If we drive the change we want to see, everyone will win.

Selling versus Guiding

While my experience with Sam and Rebecca shows how much we can help our clients, it also demonstrates how much more could be done in so many other situations. I helped a family avoid financial disaster and preserve their lifestyle, but this example still only reflects the beginning of the most holistic, integrated planning I could have helped them put in place. The only reason we got as far as we did was because we sat down together to focus on potential concerns far into the future, and I took the time to fully explain the maximum potential of their insurance portfolio.

I still regret not taking a more comprehensive approach with this family, beyond helping them with one insurance plan. This, in part, comes down to the parameters of that networking group where I met Sam. In those meetings, I held the "life insurance seat," meaning that while I operated as a full financial planner in my day-to-day business, I was asked to limit my scope to insurance in that group. Unfortunately, this perpetuates the negative compound impact of being forced to promote transactional business isolated from integrated, holistic planning.

Had Sam lived, I would have continued to hound him until they agreed to turn their focus toward building wealth for the future. At least we managed to take care of basic security first. Had we approached this in the opposite order, working through the more exciting investment strategies and putting off the life insurance, Rebecca would have been forced to make do with, at most, a small investment portfolio, which, even at maximum savings rate and maximum investment returns, still could not have come anywhere close to providing even the $500,000 of insurance they sought, let alone the $3 million they obtained.

When you're just out there selling stuff, you ask yourself questions like, "What did the client ask for and what relevant products do I have?" You worry about how interesting these solutions may seem or how smart you look. But when you truly guide your clients, the question instead becomes, "What's the very best I can do to take care of this client, and where do we start?"

When you're trapped in the first mentality, the only way for you to reach your full potential impact would be for a client to walk in your door and say, "I want to know what's the very best you can do for me." However, with public perception so low, good luck encountering that request out in the field.

If we could better motivate people to action, what might be the impact? Forty-three percent of Americans said they did not seek financial advice in 2023,[22] so what would be the impact

[22] James Royal, "Here's the top place Americans get financial advice—even young Americans," Bankrate, December 21, 2023, https://www.bankrate.com/investing/financial-advisors/americans-financial-advice-top-place/#:~:text=Despite%20these%20numbers%2C%2043%20percent,from%2C%20by%20age%20and%20income.

of these people seeking answers to even one question or taking just the first step?

Thankfully for his family, Sam trusted me enough to dramatically revise his life insurance plan. But if he hadn't had such a net negative view of our business, he wouldn't have started out by saying, "I want $500,000." He would have instead asked me, his friend and advisor, "What should I do?" Then, he might have actually taken my advice.

There's a huge difference between what Sam wanted and what he bought—six times better, to be exact. Had he known what the future had in store for him, I have no doubt he would have purchased every bit of insurance he could, which would have been twelve times more than he'd asked for and twice what his family received.

Proactive versus Reactive

So, how do we get to that intangible place where client trust can really blossom? Where more clients implement every bit of the plans we carefully craft and recommend? One way we do that is by connecting with them earlier and in a more proactive way. Just as most people build relationships with primary care physicians and go to well visits before facing major health problems, we want people to have financial advising relationships before urgent needs arise.

When something goes wrong financially in people's lives, they instantly want to solve the problem, but it's rarely possible to solve the problem after the fact. Whether we are talking about trying to obtain life or disability insurance when you are already ill or trying to save for retirement when the runway is impossibly short, our options diminish the longer we wait.

What is the potential impact of this? If the research is right, we face somewhere between a $6.8 trillion and $14 trillion retirement gap in the United States, and the average age of a client with a financial advisor is 59.4.[23] If we could earn a better reputation, change public perception, and lower the average age of our clients, what would that mean for those deficits? I don't need a calculator to know that it would be immense.

The reality is that everyone has a retirement plan, a legacy plan, and a financial plan, either by design or by default. Most just have no idea what their plan-by-default looks like until it happens—in a reactive way. They didn't *choose* it if they didn't take proactive measures to build it. If we could help more people design proactive plans, we could protect more families and begin closing the gap on that retirement savings deficit. The benefit would be immeasurable and so meaningful to the lives of countless Americans.

Sometimes I hear clients express an aversion to gambling, but when they reject the notion of planning for the future, they are literally gambling on their futures. They've bought a lottery ticket when they could have done so much more. Now, I hate to point fingers, but we're not so much better

[23] Cheryl Winokur Munk, "7 Reasons DIY Investors Should Consider Getting a Financial Advisor in 2024, Barron's, january 2, 2024, https://www.barrons.com/advisor/articles/7-reasons-diy-investors-should-consider-getting-a-financial-advisor-in-2024-bbc3f106#:~:text=assets%20with%20them.-,As%20of%20year%2Dend%202022%2C%20Cerulli%20estimates%20the%20average%20age,U.S.%20Census%20Bureau%2C%20Cerulli%20said; Nari Rhee, "The Retirement Savings Crisis: Is It Worse Than We Think?," National Institute on Retirement Security, June 2013, https://www.nirsonline.org/reports/the-retirement-savings-crisis-is-it-worse-than-we-think/#:~:text=The%20collective%20retirement%20savings%20gap,on%20working%20until%20age%2067.

ourselves. As it turns out, 70 percent of top performing advisors have a business plan, but only 28 percent of *all* advisors have business plans.[24]

What would that impact be if we all had business plans as advisors—if we all were our own best clients? How many more clients might follow our lead if we got honest with ourselves about our responsibilities? How would it impact new advisors' learning curves and confidence levels to have individualized plans for becoming independently driven towards their goals? Could it help achieving our goals feel probable—or even certain—rather than just possible? I happen to think so.

I can relate this reactive approach to my own casual risk-taking when working out. As I write this, I'm preparing for my third half marathon, still a few months away. Admittedly, I took the (ill-advised) "weekend warrior" approach all winter, going to the gym Saturdays and Sundays and pushing so hard I needed afternoon naps, then not doing much of anything for the next five days. Meanwhile, I'd also been slacking on warm-up and cool-down stretching. As a result, I recently came home from my outdoor training regimen, made a sudden turn, and felt my back go *pop*. I was out of commission for a few days while that healed.

Of course, I knew intellectually that stretching helps prevent injuries. But I grew complacent about it because, so far, I had not experienced any negative outcomes from not doing it. Everything was going just fine—until it wasn't.

[24] "5 Key Elements to a Financial Advisor Business Plan," AssetMark, October 28, 2022, https://www.assetmark.com/blog/key-elements-financial-advisor-business-plan.

I can recall countless examples of clients who, when I asked about their prior experience with financial planning, said, "We didn't have an advisor because everything seemed fine . . . until now." They hadn't taken the time to protect against what could go wrong—until it became glaringly obvious that something wasn't right. With our help, such clients can bounce back and set themselves up for better outcomes moving forward. But imagine the overall impact we could have if the majority of the public thought about us as "primary care" guidance for their financial health. If they got the financial equivalent of their bloodwork, baseline tests, and vaccines well before there was any true risk.

One way to influence this change in your practice is to expand your reach beyond older, high net worth individuals to also engage the younger, less affluent people in your community. Granted, you may need fewer solutions and touch points with younger clients, as they have less capital to make decisions about. However, those early decisions around savings plans and investments can create enormous ripples down the line—if they know all the information. They're unlikely to achieve maximum impact through Google searches or plugging info into some robo-advisor chatbot. Plus, in engaging younger community members, you'll create a client pipeline for later, when their decisions carry more financial weight.

What if we looked at the first interaction with a young prospective client as just the beginning of a long-term relationship? What if we developed more capacity for patience? What if we truly focused on becoming the center of our communities through education and others-focused relationship building? What might be the impact of that?

This represents quite the shift, for both advisors and clients. Young people with more modest assets typically manage their own finances, but there comes a point where they decide that outsourcing the labor makes more sense. This relates to many aspects of life. When I bought my first townhome, I cleaned it myself because I deemed it more important to save money. As my earnings increased, my time and energy became more professionally valuable. If the amount of time it takes you to clean your house each week in "billable hours" equates to $500 an hour, then if you do it yourself when you could be working, you're essentially paying $500 an hour to get your house cleaned. Whether people think of it in those terms or not, that's often when people start outsourcing this domestic support: when their hourly rate exceeds that of the person they can hire. Seeking professional help doesn't mean you lack the intelligence or skills to get something done yourself. It's more about people's capacity to put in the time and energy, as well as the opportunity costs of using that time and energy differently.

This concept doesn't just apply to the wealthiest members of society, nor only to people whose "net worth" qualifies them to work with fiduciaries. Regardless of a client's current situation, we as advisors can tailor fit a plan to their unique situation and goals and help them go much further than they'd be able to go alone. When we wait until someone acquires half a million dollars or more before popping in to say, "I can help you now!" our clients lose out on decades of potential compound impact. Rather than paying attention to how much wealth they have accumulated up to that point, look at how you can be most valuable to them—and when. This includes developing the planning as early as possible. Overall, that's the biggest difference between client-centered and transactional advising—measuring a client by your ability to help, versus by how much you will earn (fiduciary title or not, if you are focused solely on the amount of money in the transaction, it's still transactional).

If advisors can truly shift from the competitive, transactional mindset to one of improving lives through compound impact, we can focus on much more than sales numbers and rates of return. We can talk to clients about safeguarding standards of living and increasing generational wealth through ensuring their family's upward mobility. To me, generational wealth is not just about millionaires becoming billionaires. It reflects an aspiration that any and *every* family can achieve with the right planning: for the next generation to live better than the last.

Myth of "Overinsured"

When graduating physicians receive their white coats, they take the Hippocratic Oath to "first, do no harm." We need to bring this emphasis on harm reduction into our work as financial advisors. One way to do that is to make sure clients understand the implications of both inaction and partial action—compared to the potential positive impact we can help them secure.

So many clients express irrational suspicions around insurance. They feel like they're being "oversold" or "overinsured." Some reject the notion of discussing it at all, feeling like we're encouraging them to "profit" from the potential death of their loved ones. But insurance is all about *replacing* what's lost—and avoiding compound disaster—not about profits. It's about holding your place in line as your family moves through the stages of education and wealth building on the journey toward their American Dream. For my family, the journey began when my great grandparents immigrated to Canada as farmers. One of my grandfathers drove a gravel truck and the other worked as a prison guard. My parents owned a furniture store, and now my son is on his way to becoming an engineer. We all work toward something, and using a robust financial plan to "hold our place in line" helps us ensure that every generation lives better than the last.

Recently, I had to tap into my car insurance when someone tried to park and miscalculated, destroying the front of my brand-new car. The other driver had great insurance, and so did I. Yet, I still had to tap into my personal funds to find a certified dealer to properly restore my car to its original state.

While there's a difference between the products we sell and both car and health insurance models, this anecdote illustrates the myth that we can be "overinsured." Again, insurance provides the function of replacing what's lost, and it too often falls short of that goal, mainly when people fail to accurately calculate the value of the asset they are insuring. However much I may want to, I couldn't insure my car for twice its value.

Rate of Savings Impact

It's easy to see how a multi-million-dollar insurance policy ensures better outcomes than the $500,000 plan. We can apply the same logic to wealth management. Too often, advisors view this aspect of financial advising in terms of market-based returns alone. There's undoubtedly an impact from securing a better rate of return, better tax status, or increased diversification. But, to me, that's the wealth management equivalent of selling the $500,000 term policy rather than educating clients on the very best they can do. It's a small impact that's helpful to clients, and it certainly does no harm.

However, we need to talk more about the immense value of maximizing clients' rate of savings over their lifetime, as well as beginning to save earlier, because the compound impact of those two things—even if people stick their money in a box in their backyard—typically far outweigh the impact of portfolio changes to a single lump sum of money. (Please don't put your money in a box in the backyard).

The wealth management sector tends to center their entire approach around security selection and timing. While they may not be causing harm, this approach ignores the broader implications, reducing people's entire lives to market shares. Meanwhile, their clients are thinking about how to build businesses, finance loans, buy homes and cars, save for their kids' college, and still manage to retire one day. Too many advisors focus the bulk of their attention on the investments themselves and not nearly enough on the strategies linked to improving savings rates. This leaves their clients out there making all these vital financial decisions (and often mistakes) alone.

According to the Unbiased 2023 Financial Confidence Survey, only 25 percent of adults consider themselves extremely financially confident.[25] As an industry, there's so much more we can do to help increase that number. What would be the impact if we did a more complete job?

If you ask me, waiting for clients to achieve a certain net worth before reaching out to form relationships amounts to

---

[25] Rachel Carey, "Financial confidence in the US," Unbiased, October 5, 2023, https://www.unbiased.com/discover/financial-advice/financial-confidence-in-the-us.

partial action at best. We miss so many opportunities to educate people about the invaluable impact of earlier savings plans. Where does the $6.8 to 14 trillion retirement savings deficit come from? In large part, it comes from advisors not taking the time to do the whole job. It comes from the public's severe lack of trust in us and from how we interact with them and approach our work. All of that compounds into an impact deficit.

Slow Down to Speed Up

As it turns out, this earthy, crunchy idea of actually *caring* profits both clients and advisors. It builds the trust we need to guide our clients toward success. It also allows us to fully tune into our clients and understand their needs, desires, and challenges. When you get to know your clients in depth and holistically, you're much better poised to make a greater impact.

Without the years-long relationship I'd built with Sam, he would have ignored my request to meet with his wife, assumed I was just trying to line my own pockets, and bought his $500,000 life insurance plan from a less thorough advisor, or even online.

In hindsight, it's easy to see the impact of such trust and engagement, particularly in the case of Rebecca and her children. Still, advisors often push back when I urge them to slow down and focus on relationship building, arguing that they're not "taking care of business," presumably by closing a sale and earning money for themselves. By taking this short-term view, they miss out on opportunities for much greater, if longer-term, rewards for everyone involved.

You can test your mindset by examining whether you're more likely to take your time and get things right when meeting with older, more affluent clients, compared to younger people who are just getting started. If you feel yourself rushing through the latter, ask yourself: Why? Given what we know about the compound impact of setting up responsible savings plans as early as possible, why not get excited about the opportunity to make such a vast difference in the lives of these younger clients? Why not invest in early financial education and guidance, laying the groundwork for a lifetime of better decision-making?

When your business is truly flourishing and you have run out of open appointments, why not pay it forward by offering mentorship and referrals to a younger advisor? Have you ever called a doctor who can't take on new patients? They tend to mention a colleague who's able to help you out. Newer advisors can build relationships with incoming clients who reach out for your team's advice, forging a future for themselves and helping ensure your practice will truly leave a legacy.

There's immense value for advisors and firms in building strong early relationships that may not result in large transactions right away but have the potential to pay out down the road in terms of client loyalty, trust, and a cascade of referrals. If you feel that you can't afford this approach, in terms of taking your time to lay a solid foundation for your career, you're probably not ready for this work—or maybe it's simply not the right profession for you.

I say this because you potentially do far more harm by rushing than by slowing down to get things right. If you're in a rush to build clients just for today, without an eye on the future, you're less likely to build the rapport you need to retain those clients, let alone secure a lifelong relationship with clients who trust you with their whole world (and all the future referrals that tend to come along with that). Instead, you'll end up spinning your wheels. When the clients you rushed through gain some years of experience and a bigger paycheck, they'll look for a more seasoned advisor to do their more significant planning—someone who really cares.

Yes, it's important to maintain forward momentum. But if you take the time to really focus on your clients, that trust you build will do the hard work for you. When it comes to things like getting life insurance or setting up a savings plan, time pressure and fear-based tactics rarely work. Instead, motivate people to act by getting them talking about what they value and where they want to be. There's tremendous value in simply getting clients to finally do what they already know they need to do, and they're much more likely to get there when they have an established relationship with a trusted advisor. That's when your efforts at early engagement pay huge dividends. That's when they start taking 100 percent of your advice.

Accountability & Self-Analysis

When clients decline to take all or part of our advice, we need to examine what went wrong. We won't get better unless we acknowledge and analyze mistakes, failures, and missed opportunities—and make an attempt to measure the cost. Are you holding yourself responsible for the impact you *could* have had? Are you taking account of what's left on the table? If not, how can you evaluate your own potential, let alone achieve it? It's not easy to admit when you fall short. But if you're truly centering your clients and community, you have to hold yourself accountable.

What would be the impact of changing your measuring stick to one based on impact rather than how you compare to your peers? What if you shifted your metrics from income earned to families helped, protections placed, systematic savings added, plans implemented, and relationships built?

What would happen if you worked *with* your clients rather than *for* yourself? How would that affect your confidence, the pride you take in your work, and the resulting compound curve of both your impact and your earnings?

If we all adopted a true growth mindset based on the right things, it would be felt throughout the profession and throughout society as a win for everyone involved.

I'm relieved I could help Rebecca and her children avoid the destabilizing outcome of downsizing their whole lives after Sam's death. Still, I pursue this ideal of compound impact because I know that in a different environment, with a different public attitude toward planning, I could have done much more—$3 million more, to be exact. At least I can rest easier knowing I went out of my way to explain and encourage the most optimal outcome—and that I made a significant positive impact compared to where this family would be without my guidance. It's never my job to write the check or make decisions for clients, but it is my responsibility to share with them the best they can do.

It's also my responsibility to ask myself how I might have done better. Every time.

When people hear "client impact" from a financial advisor, they may be thinking about a linear impact, on either the advisor's practice or the client's portfolio. What I'm talking about goes much further than a higher investment return or the growth of an advisor's practice. Sometimes, with one single transaction, we can help a family preserve their home and quality of life, continue saving for their kids' college funds, and maintain continuity, stability, and community. If you ask me, that's true legacy. That's what compound impact is all about.

GUT CHECK

Did you at least *present* 100 percent of the best solution? If not, what did you leave out and why?

Are you selling or guiding? How can you improve your approach?

Have you been proactive in your own planning?

What does your portfolio of "next gen" clients look like?

CHAPTER 10

IMPACT *for* LEADERS

Nearly 80 percent of Americans reported living paycheck to paycheck in 2023, according to a Payroll.org survey.[26] That doesn't mean everybody's struggling, but it does suggest that eight out of ten Americans feel stuck where they are, unable to advance. Meanwhile, our industry churns through financial advisors at four-year retention rates of just 15 percent, which only aggravates that trend.

A lot of people may read this book and think, "We make a difference every day helping clients. This problem related to public perception and national advisor retention is really not my problem." While both of these things may be technically true, I am exhausted by this type of thinking.

I am invigorated and inspired by the thought of the impact we could have if we were able to change those retention rates. If more advisors succeeded, that would mean more Americans advancing in their financial goals. The two go hand in hand.

---

[26] Emily Batdorf, "Living Paycheck to Paycheck Statistics 2024," *Forbes* Advisor, April 2, 2024, https://www.forbes.com/advisor/banking/living-paycheck-to-paycheck-statistics-2024/.

Think of the ripple effect of increasing advisor retention. Imagine how much more effectively and efficiently we could grow our businesses if we increased advisor retention from 15 to 70 percent or beyond. Theoretically, you could invest exactly the same amount of money into new advisors and gain almost five times the compound effect on both your impact and your bottom line. I'm no actuary, but I would think pure productivity alone would increase by 400 percent, not to mention a reduction in recruiting, onboarding, and training costs and an increase in client satisfaction. Those ripple effects would also include faster growth for your firm and more opportunities for new advisors to learn from greater numbers of more experienced colleagues.

When leaders in our field talk about developing and scaling firms, we almost exclusively talk in terms of recruiting. In particular, I hear a lot about "volume recruiting"—this idea that you have to talk to one hundred people to get fifty first interviews and twenty-five second interviews, all for one hire.

Not only is this extremely inefficient, it's also clearly ineffectual. We're casting too wide a net to recruit mainly salespeople with little interest in client impact, while neglecting to address the fact that how we do business drives out 85 percent of those recruits within four years. That's not because of them, it's because of us. We picked them, and we owe them the leadership and training they need to thrive.

By improving retention and investing most of our energy into improving client relationships, we gain genuine financial rewards. The client-centered, impact-driven approach to financial guidance is not just selfless idealism. It's good business.

In fact, it's a game changer.

Jumping off the Cliff

At most firms, our advisors have chosen to work within a structure without a fixed, guaranteed salary. Like entrepreneurs, they're jumping off that cliff into a career where they truly earn what they're worth based on results. Unlike entrepreneurs, they also have a robust support structure, including our leadership, to help them along the way.

What feels like a disadvantage—the lack of salary and a guaranteed regular paycheck—quickly becomes a benefit to those who succeed. Rather than being paid an "average" of the revenue that you and the rest of your colleagues bring in, you get rewarded proportionately for your effectiveness. This may feel dicey at first, but it can become one of the most stable forms of employment over the long run due to the residual income earned and the strength of client relationships—if firms want to keep clients, they must also keep their advisors. That's pretty good job security. The problem that leads to our lack of retention is not the payment structure itself but that we've had the wrong idea about how to get to the "results" we need for these advisors to succeed.

For evidence, just look to the business practices of our most successful veteran advisors. Around the country, I've met and worked with inspiring community leaders with well-established client-first mentalities. These leaders exemplify financial advising driven first by client and community impact. They've secured their right to thrive in this business for life, knowing they can stand behind the work they do.

As leaders responsible for developing new advisors, we need to also take this long view focused on ideal client outcomes.

That's not an easy thing to do, especially when you lead people just starting out in this field. Often, an initial panic (sometimes a *forever* panic) sets in. The idea that "I'm only going to get paid if I sell something" tends to lead directly into the idea that "I better go out there and close some deals—pronto." Our empathy for these advisors as they launch can result in us jumping into the trenches with them to just do *something* and stave off their inclination to give up too soon.

This can drive people to obsess over lead generation and dive into cold-calling in order to find somebody—anybody—who wants to buy what they're selling. As we know, that's not true advising; it's just product sales. This approach quickly leads to advisor burnout and reinforces the high advisor turnover that stifles growth and undermines client trust. We will never retain the majority of our advisors for more than four years with old methodology.

Not only does the transactional approach perpetuate our negative public reputation, but it also fails to build both loyalty in clients and an advisor's reputation in the community. We have to put our time and energy into training our advisors to work with people, not just with products. If the marketplace perceives our value as just another retail product provider, why would consumers come to us when they can just shop online themselves?

A recent TechCrunch article[27] highlighted various fintech failures that attempted to automate elements of financial

[27] Grant Easterbrook, "10 years of fintech failure: 3 more ideas that failed to live up to the initial hype," TechCrunch, April 24, 2023, https://techcrunch.com/2023/04/24/10-years-of-fintech-failure-3-more-ideas-that-failed-to-live-up-to-the-initial-hype/.

advising, from financial planning apps to algorithm-based advice. The hype of the fintech industry has thankfully not dramatically changed how we engage with our clients—though it has tried and tried. At least for now, real live humans are still the preferred choice for Americans seeking a financial advisor. If we handle this reality appropriately, I believe we will remain the preferred choice.

Our popularity over robo-advising should give us cause for optimism. We need to have faith in ourselves and in our ability to change this industry and make this incredible impact. Like our new advisors, we need to trust ourselves enough to step off the "cliff" of the old ways and build new solid ground underfoot.

We need to train our advisors to prioritize client progress over their own quick results. We have to insist on transparency; what we say we do in classrooms has to match what we say we do in the field.

We also have to measure our progress as leaders in terms of our advisors' impact and ability to succeed independently, without us swooping in to play the hero and transact on their behalf.

In these ways and more, what would be the impact of more regularly and seriously questioning your own status quo?

To have the greatest impact on our clients and for our firms, we need to change the focus from our company's bottom line and our own performance as a leader and really focus on our advisors. The sum of the whole is only truly greater than the sum of its parts when you take the time to invest into and develop those parts.

Others-Focused Recruiting—for the Long Haul

When we make our leadership about elevating the team (rather than enriching ourselves or gratifying our own egos), we promote a different energy and a new synergy.

We do that by finding people who can align with an impact-driven philosophy, not just those whom you relate to and get along with. Stop looking through the lens of yourself—what glorifies you, as the leader—and hire for the future instead.

When people can see their future in your firm, they will come. Be intentional about how you will help people build their careers. Take interest in who they are as people and help them connect what they love with what they do for a living. Emphasize the relationships they will build and the impact they will make as a result, all while building a successful career.

When thinking through the lens of impact, it becomes clear that personality-driven leadership is not the one-size-fits-all solution to our problems. We need to expand the number of people who can advise and become leaders in their own right, and when you believe everything must go through you as the owner of all knowledge and the savior of financial problems, your organization can't scale.

Traditionally, we've spent an awful lot of time pounding our chests and showing off our success.

It should be no surprise that those advisors and leaders who never settle for less than 100 percent of what they can do for clients often rise to the top. Unfortunately, they still feel like outliers. In fact, they often end up separating themselves from the pack, disengaging from larger organizations, and launching their own practices, mainly because they don't align with how their larger organizations operated. In other words, they become great impact-driven advisors on their own—not *because of* how we attract, recruit, hire, train, and lead, but *in spite* of it.

Meanwhile, too many people who could have followed in their footsteps either never become attracted to our field in the first place, or they get demoralized and drop out. They look at how our industry functions overall and just decide, "You know what? This isn't for me."

Beyond Trophies

For the culture to truly change—for advisors to shift to an authentic drive toward impact—we need to reward both advisors and leaders for the right things. The next time you attend an awards program, turn around once in a while to witness the body language of the audience. What percentage of the room looks engaged, motivated, or inspired by what's going on?

When I look around at these events, I always see and hear the same thing: a lot of people on their phones, spouses wishing they didn't have to be there, and conversations centered around whether or not the handful of people getting the same awards year after year have lost weight or changed hairstyles.

Alternatively, imagine the impact of celebrating the most meaningful impact of our work through recognition that actually energizes and inspires us all.

Instead, we award income and revenue, devoid of its impact or meaning. What does this look like from the outside? How would clients feel watching us celebrate our own narrowly defined "success"? Do we look like an industry that cares about our clients? Does that inspire public trust? Just imagine if doctors behaved like we do—hosting award ceremonies focused not on client outcomes but on their individual revenue in relation to their colleagues.

Advising should not be about personal gains and winning trophies. To help the majority of the general public break their paycheck-to-paycheck stagnation and achieve what matters most to their financial health, we need a much deeper thought process. This is about people's lives, their families, and their future generations—not about some transactional, short-term "winner" (much less "killer") mentality. (And for those of you who love the trophies—don't worry. I'm not saying we can't have trophies. I'm just challenging us to award them based on a different set of metrics.)

We absolutely should measure and reward advisor progress by looking at results, annual growth metrics, and tiers of productivity. But when doing so, let's take a more critical lens and consider whether or not we'd be proud to have our best clients in the room with us. Could this be a fist bump *with* clients, or is it strictly one for behind closed doors?

This is also not to say we have to swing dramatically in the opposite direction and train our people to behave like therapists, only asking questions and avoiding assertive answers. Advisors must be direct, engage in difficult conversations, and guide clients toward something greater. They need to solve problems and motivate clients to take action for their own financial success. This cannot be a passive experience.

The other day, I interviewed an advisor candidate currently working at another firm. She shared her accolades for hitting sales targets, explaining the timelines for each. At one point, she said to me, "I know there are clients who should really do more than what I am recommending, but right now I'm on a timeline, and I need to just get the win."

What does it mean when our incentives for good work actively *discourage* advisors from doing the best work possible for the clients and the industry? If we're training people to worry about their own short-term targets and *disincentivizing* the best long-term client care, we undercut every element laid out in this book.

The reality is that once an advisor has a steady pipeline of prospects, business does not slow down at all. If there are enough projects in motion, there's always something ready to cross the finish line. But when advisor habits are not healthy and consistent enough to generate that activity, they're left without enough to do. That's when they get tempted to take shortcuts.

In almost every client interaction, we reach a tipping point at which it would be easier just to say to clients, "Sure, we can do what you want" and transact. It takes time and energy to add, "But let me help you understand what else might be possible and why what you're thinking may not be the very best decision." Or, if you must, "Let's start there but also schedule time to meet again to look at your overall potential beyond this one solution."

As leaders, we need to offer advisors plans to generate consistent quality interactions with prospective clients. In demonstrating business plans and approaches we believe in, we will get our people on board.

If you're building business plans for an advisor who wants to generate a certain income by AUM (because that is the personal outcome they desire), challenge them to go further. What type of products and in what marketplace are they likely to find these sales? From there, build a plan to get your advisor in front of that market and measure your effectiveness in terms of building relationships within it. Have them set the goal of meeting with a certain number of people within that market each week to introduce their value. If they look for the relationships and build trust, the sales will follow. They will generate better results if sales become the natural outcomes of a main focus on relationships. Meanwhile, your advisors will gain control of their businesses and be able to predict their results with much more certainty.

I truly believe that if we, as an industry, can start making the changes laid out in this book, we'll start to attract and retain more of the right people. We'll find ourselves surrounded by advisors who earn client trust and put in the work to ensure they do a complete job, which will help change public opinion of our field. Meanwhile, those candidates only motivated by competition and money will find something else to sell.

Representation, Diversity, and Impact

What does diversity really look like in your community? Next time you walk into a local supermarket, look around and ask yourself, "Do the demographics of my advisors reflect my community?" While I think we're making progress on this front, we're still woefully far from adequately representing our consumer base.

What would happen to our market penetration if our client base reflected our communities more fully? How much more could we achieve if this representation extended to our advisor populations, leadership teams, and the results on our leaderboards?

If we truly care about improving the financial lives of all Americans, we need to address this problem. That begins with attracting the right people to the business. Even if we adjust our recruiting ads and interview processes and manage to get the right people in the door, are they going to feel comfortable with how we train, reward, and mentor people?

Too many organizations still operate according to an outdated model that assumes there is only one way to work: the way it's always been. Naturally, this favors the recruits who feel at home in this type of structure and disadvantages others. For me, this showed up in the form of the locked door at the morning training session. For others, it may be something different.

Especially since COVID-19, more people prioritize the flexibility of working from home and setting their own hours, for all kinds of reasons. I've worked with advisors who care for aging parents and people with early-morning commitments related to their faith, to name a few. The reality is that if we want to be competitive and attract the very best talent to our firms, we must learn to adapt. In very meaningful ways, our advisors are our clients too. Think about the lengths you would go to make things convenient and accessible to your clients. Are you doing the same for your advisors?

I have heard people argue that the newer, younger people coming into the business can't work remotely because they lack discipline. I don't buy it. If somebody wants to work from home, they must have the capacity to be organized and self-motivated, and if they're not, they shouldn't be in the business. We won't evolve by trying a new strategy one time, then giving up. To truly adapt, we need to experiment and iterate until we get it right.

We can no longer force advisors into some outdated mold, especially one with clearly diminishing returns. Instead, it's time to hang our ears on the bell, taking into account the very real experiences and issues facing the people we hire. That's the essence of the "dream manager" approach. There's no reason why we can't attract and retain advisors who better represent our communities. There's no reason why we can't train people in ways that complement their lives rather than complicating them. If we truly care about having the greatest compound impact on more clients, advisors, organizations, and communities, we have to be able to adapt.

We also must become clear on why we're doing this and how. True workplace diversity is not about just meeting some hiring quota. To address the wealth gap inherent in more demographically diverse communities, we need to actually engage with these communities. Better representation certainly helps, but it's not enough to simply hire diverse advisors. We have to also retain these advisors and build them into *leaders* who can make a real impact in communities. We won't see more diversity on our leaderboards until we figure out how to retain, mentor, and develop diverse candidates—for every role in the business.

Let's also talk about *all* underserved communities. Looking at the geography of the United States, you see so many rural areas far from big metropolitan centers. These communities also need financial advisors, and they likely can't get into an office in a city center somewhere.

If our industry really cared about client and community impact, we would see a concerted effort to engage more with underserved communities of all kinds. That means moving away from the elite image of the trophy-winning, superstar advisor raking in the profits. It means investing in strategies that allow our field to morph into something that truly guides and supports all Americans.

It seems likely to me that, as an advisor, your earnings typically resemble those of the clients you work with. If you mainly engage clients who earn $50,000 a year, you'll probably earn between $50,000 and $75,000 a year, and if you mainly work with clients earning half a million, you'll likewise land in that general area yourself. There are clear outliers, of course, such as people who specialize in a specific field and have a very high-volume business. But overall, this line of thinking likely holds. It's wonderful for people to work with very successful clients and earn a lot of money. However, we need to also support people in lower income areas who would be content to earn a livable wage providing invaluable guidance that uplifts these communities.

Rural physicians make less than those in urban centers, but these communities still have family doctors. While these professionals could simply move to a city and earn more, they remain. Why? Because, in addition to considerations about quality of life, they likely care about the patients and communities they serve. I see no reason why our field of financial advising couldn't also reflect and thrive within more diverse ecosystems. But we won't get there as long as our industry remains an elite, gatekept space that overlooks and ignores lower- to middle-income Americans in favor of the already wealthy. Unless we add this demographic to our client portfolio, negative public opinion of our field will continue to sour.

Past the Threshold of Change

It's important to realize that I'm not asking us to choose between short-term profits and long-term profitability. The latter begets the former pretty quickly. It's all about getting past that threshold of change to fulfill our industry's full potential and have the greatest impact. When the pipeline is full, it's full. It shouldn't matter whether any one client interaction takes days or months to complete. With enough people interested in your help, there will always be someone crossing the finish line.

True engagement—the kind that drives compound impact—builds on relationships, not purchases. When you're more integrated into your clients' lives, trust runs deeper. Statistically, 70 percent of women leave their financial advisor after the death of their spouse.[28] Our industry has learned the hard way that the client who makes financial decisions today will not necessarily control that wealth forever. The papercuts formed by ignoring the spouse and neglecting the kids run deep. By 2030, an estimated $30 trillion dollars of wealth will transfer to spouses and other beneficiaries.[29] If the 70-percent attrition trend among survivors holds true, most firms and advisors will pay the cost of an outdated approach of directing all their focus on the breadwinner.

---

[28] "The Future of Wealth Is Female," Integrated Resources Inc., https://www.iri-online.org/wp-content/uploads/legacy/default-document-library/272669_0121_women-and-investing-white-paper_final_021021-update_digital.pdf.

[29] Pooneh Baghai, Olivia Howard, Lakshmi Prakash, and Jill Zucker, "Women as the next wave of growth in US wealth management, McKinsey & Company, July 29, 2020, https://www.mckinsey.com/industries/financial-services/our-insights/women-as-the-next-wave-of-growth-in-us-wealth-management.

I'm not saying we need to "make ourselves part of the family," because that would be disingenuous. We can, however, become a profession that entire families can truly rely on.

Sometimes, getting past that threshold of change can feel like quicksand, but that's mainly due to our own misconceptions and blind spots. So much of the resistance stems from this false idea that it's better or easier to model your business on what's "worked" for decades rather than sticking your neck out and adapting.

When your clients feel heard and cared for, they're far more likely to take your advice. I know this because I evaluate my own effectiveness based on how often clients implement the advice I give them. I only recommend what I fully believe to be in their best interest, so it follows that when I'm at my best, they don't just implement part of my solutions, but rather 100 percent of them. My clients typically insure the full value of their incomes, they save 20 percent or more of their gross annual income, and they diversify their investments between safe liquid options—those that are opportunistic but tax-advantaged—and retirement plans blending guaranteed income with tax-deferred growth. This stance may seem oversimplified to some, but both in terms of pure performance and compound impact, the results outperform the average financial plan, according to research by Ernst & Young Global Limited (EY).[30]

---

[30] Justin Singer, "How life insurers can provide differentiated retirement benefits," EY.com, October 10, 2022, https://www.ey.com/en_us/insights/insurance/how-life-insurers-can-provide-differentiated-retirement-benefits.

Finally, we can measure this evolution in terms of how many unsolicited client referrals our advisors receive, as well as unsolicited advisor candidate referrals coming to us. As they say, success leaves clues.

Far from threatening the profitability of our work, the client-centered approach emerges as our best strategy for lifting consumers out of the paycheck-to-paycheck cycle[31] and enriching their lives, as well as ourselves, our advisors, and our industry as a whole.

GUT CHECK

Are you selecting advisors with the capacity to succeed?

Are you showing people how their future could look within your firm?

What metrics and results are you rewarding?

How many different strategies have you tried to improve your diversity? Have you looked for help?

Are you willing to move beyond the threshold of change?

[31] To remove any biases you may have, I have seen people making seven figures and still living paycheck to paycheck due to poor money management.

CONCLUSION

While Albert Einstein is often attributed with calling compound interest the "eighth wonder of the world," he was probably only kind of joking. The difference between linear and exponential growth can seem outright miraculous. That same principle applies to the impact of our work—both in terms of what we do and in terms of what we leave undone.

When advisors hawk isolated, Band-Aid solutions, it's often due to short-term, linear thinking. Typically, they're trying to add up sales dollars to meet their weekly, monthly, or quarterly goals. This not only keeps advisors stuck on hamster wheels (perpetuating our dismal retention rates), but it also shortchanges both our clients' financial futures and the reputation of our field overall.

Moving forward, we cannot build successful careers and thriving practices by adding up transactions and profits in some linear way. We should do it instead by hanging our ears on the bell—by thinking first and foremost about our clients' best interests. Then, we can get their houses in order, starting with the foundation: Do they have adequate income protection in place? How much are they saving each month? Are their investments optimized to their needs and situations?

Asking questions like these—and taking the time to truly consider the best answers—may not earn you every week's top sales trophy. But it will earn you the trust of clients, colleagues, and community members and the lasting career rewards that come with it.

That kind of trust leads to lifelong relationships with clients who actually take your advice to safeguard their assets and improve their financial outcomes, while sharing your name with everyone they know. Meanwhile, by authentically engaging with your communities, you'll gain robust networks of professionals who come to you for advice and happily send introductions and referrals your way.

I'm not just talking about building a personal pipeline of clients. This approach will also set you up to become an industry leader whose impact ripples out through every advisor, mentor, and coach—and through every client and community member impacted by their work.

If enough leaders take this others-focused approach, we can increase the quality of applicants and help our advisors stay, and thrive, in this industry, allowing us to shift strategic effort and resources away from constant recycled recruitment patterns and instead toward scaling our firms' growth and expanding our impact even more.

It will take a sea change to substantially improve our industry's reputation—not to mention decrease the US retirement savings deficit, protect more families against unforeseen consequences, and enrich the lives of all Americans through earlier, more accessible, and more impact-driven guidance. I believe we can get there, but it won't be by following the old playbook on how to advise, hire, train, or lead.

I know that such huge, systematic changes can feel unrealistic and out of reach, but that's only when we think in linear terms rather than appreciating the exponential compound impact of sincere and consistent engagement rooted in positive change.

Growth over "Perfection"

I don't have to tell you that the road we're traveling together is riddled with potholes and speed bumps. There's an awful lot of uphill climb to go before that first glorious downhill stretch.

Luckily, along my journey, I've been blessed with friends, mentors, and advocates who could "speak Amy." About a year and half into my journey, at my first awards conference, one woman in particular zeroed in on me within the small crowd. She was the head of leadership development in our system at the time, and she thought I had something worth cultivating. She became a mentor, advocate and, ultimately, a dear friend. While this woman witnessed my successes, she also witnessed the bumps, bruises, and broken bones experienced along the way (not all of them mine).

I recall one leadership awards conference where I led my team in a sandcastle building competition. Before the buzzer even sounded to start the contest, my incredible leadership skills had inspired my team to mutiny. (*Oops.* Also, *ouch*).

In spite of this—and some other stories too embarrassing to even share—this mentor eventually approached me to ask if I'd be willing to serve as her own personal financial advisor. I accepted, deeply honored by her request.

You see, there is no such thing as "perfection" in our business. There is, however, a whole lot of growth. Not the kind that cuts corners to maintain your streak of sales "wins," but the kind that—if enough of us make the right changes—can expand our industry's reach and deepen our impact.

Similarly, the impact-driven approach doesn't guarantee some "perfect" outcome in advance; it simply means consistently putting our clients and advisors in the most optimal positions possible. It means understanding that it truly is a deep honor to be entrusted with what we do—every single time.

Toward the Tipping Point

For those of us at the tip of this spear, the journey can be frustrating. It might feel like our efforts aren't making a broader difference, especially when we see so many advisors and leaders still following the old, outdated playbook rather than taking action to make positive changes that could dramatically impact so many. But I think the reality is that most people are simply on autopilot, still unaware that they're following faulty logic. Maybe they've never felt compelled to think critically about what they're doing. Maybe they don't feel they *can* make a difference.

But there are people out there driving toward better outcomes, and a tipping point is coming, whether proactively from our industry leadership or due to a systematic industry failure to adapt to our rapidly changing world.

As an individual, you may not be able to go out and change the world at scale today, but you can plant seeds. You can approach every single client relationship and interaction with an eye toward impact. In fact, if you ask me, that is our job.

Leaders are not meant to perpetuate the status quo. That's just a glorified follower. Instead, it's our charge to lead the next generation of change. We need to understand the power of our choices and try on new perspectives. So, put yourself among the few people who critically look at our systems, step outside them, and take new action.

To achieve the kind of client-centered goals I hope we share, we need to ensure our motivations stay rooted in integrity and get carried out with transparency.

We must build trust early and often, which means listening, meeting others where they are, demonstrating humility, and getting vulnerable.

We must be truly present and engage deeply with the communities we wish to serve.

It all starts with cultivating a professional drive based on impact, building trust and authentic engagement with clients and community, and helping make a real change in the lives of others—by changing how we do things ourselves. If we can give those metrics a try, we just might move from transactions to transformations.

A tipping point—by design—is well within reach. But public perception will only change when we, as advisors and leaders, change—how we interact with our clients and the public, how we measure progress, how we hire, and how we train, coach, and mentor. *That* is our responsibility.

Every shift we make, however incremental, that helps us make clear our motivations, build genuine trust, and increase our engagement has the potential to exponentially impact the lives of our clients, colleagues, advisors, and communities.

So, Uncle Leo, it has been quite the journey, but I hope the last couple hundred pages have helped to answer your question. A question that (unfortunately) accurately reflects where we currently stand with the public—and just how far we still have to go.

As for me? I have no problem reconciling who I am as a person with the profession I'm in. And *that* is the kind of wealth I wish to share with all of you.

ACKNOWLEDGMENTS

Mike—For believing in me from the day we met. There is nothing quite like having someone in your corner every single day.

Cal—For inspiring me to leave the world a little better than I found it. I am so impressed by your confidence and your focus.

Mom—I love that you raised me to believe that there was nothing I couldn't accomplish.

Dad—Literally nothing ruffles your feathers or can sway you off your path. Thank you for the Sisu.

Emily, Danielle, Caitlin—My girls! We had to howl at the moon for this book to get written.

Jason—Thanks for being the first follower, and thank you to Mary Ellen for letting him work through his "process."

David, Andie & Nat—Thank you for being my partners and for refusing to accept the status quo every day.

Anita, Kait, and Ballast Books—Thank you for organizing my thoughts so beautifully. I have loved the process.

IMPORTANT INFORMATION

Amy Salo is a registered principal and financial advisor of Park Avenue Securities LLC (PAS). OSJ: 200 Broadhollow Road, Suite 405, Melville, NY 11747, (631) 589-5400. Securities products and advisory services offered through PAS, member FINRA, SIPC. General agent of the Guardian Life Insurance Company of America® (Guardian), New York, NY. PAS is a wholly owned subsidiary of Guardian. Forest Hills Financial Group is not an affiliate or subsidiary of PAS or Guardian. CA Insurance License Number: 0L64608.

2024-178152

This material contains the current opinions of the author but not necessarily those of the Guardian Life Insurance Company (Guardian), New York, NY, or its subsidiaries, and such opinions are subject to change without notice. The material discussed is meant for general informational purposes only and is not to be construed as tax, legal, or investment advice. Although the information has been gathered from sources believed to be reliable, please note that individual situations can vary. Therefore, the information should be relied upon only when coordinated with individual professional advice.

Guardian, its subsidiaries, agents, and employees do not give tax, legal, or accounting advice. Consult your tax, legal, or accounting professional regarding your individual situation.

By providing this content, Park Avenue Securities LLC and your financial representative are not undertaking to provide investment advice or make a recommendation for a specific individual or situation or to otherwise act in a fiduciary capacity.

All whole life insurance policy guarantees are subject to the timely payment of all required premiums and the claims paying ability of the issuing insurance company. Policy loans and withdrawals affect the guarantees by reducing the policy's death benefit and cash values.